RENAISSANCE

VOLUME 9

Religious Dissent — Tapestry

GROLIER
EDUCATIONAL

Published by Grolier Educational
Sherman Turnpike
Danbury, Connecticut 06816

Set ISBN 0-7172-5673-1
Volume 9 ISBN 0-7172-5671-5

Library of Congress Cataloging-in-Publication Data

Renaissance.
    p. cm.
Summary: Chronicles the cultural and artistic flowering
known as the Renaissance that flourished in Europe and
in other parts of the world from approximately 1375 to
1575 A.D.
Includes index.
Contents: v. 1. Africa–Bologna — v. 2. Books and libraries–
Constantinople — v. 3. Copernicus–Exploration — v. 4.
Eyck–Government — v. 5. Guilds and crafts–Landscape
painting — v. 6. Language–Merchants — v. 7. Michelangelo–
Palaces and villas — v. 8. Palestrina–Reformation — v. 9.
Religious dissent–Tapestry — v. 10. Technology–Zwingli.
    ISBN 0-7172-5673-1 (set : alk. paper)
    1. Renaissance—Juvenile literature. [1. Renaissance.]
I. Grolier Educational (Firm)
    CB361 .R367 2002
    940.2'1—dc21
                                 2002002477

For information address the publisher:
Grolier Educational, Sherman Turnpike,
Danbury, Connecticut 06816

FOR BROWN PARTWORKS

Project Editor: Shona Grimbly
Deputy Editor: Rachel Bean
Text Editors: Emily Hill
                       Jane Scarsbrook
Designer: Sarah Williams
Picture Research: Veneta Bullen
Maps: Colin Woodman
Design Manager: Lynne Ross
Production: Matt Weyland
Managing Editor: Tim Cooke
Consultant: Stephen A. McKnight
                       University of Florida

Printed and bound in Singapore

ABOUT THIS BOOK

This is one of a set of 10 books that tells the story of the Renaissance—a time of discovery and change in the world. It was during this period—roughly from 1375 to 1575—that adventurous mariners from Europe sailed the vast oceans in tiny ships and found the Americas and new sea routes to the Spice Islands of the East. The influx of gold and silver from the New World and the increase in trade made many merchants and traders in Europe extremely rich. They spent some of their wealth on luxury goods like paintings and gold and silver items for their homes, and this created a new demand for the work of artists of all kinds. Europe experienced a cultural flowering as great artists like Leonardo da Vinci, Michelangelo, and Raphael produced masterpieces that have never been surpassed.

At the same time, scholars were rediscovering the works of the ancient Greek and Roman writers, and this led to a new way of looking at the world based on observation and the importance of the individual. This humanism, together with other new ideas, spread more rapidly than ever before thanks to the development of printing with movable type.

There was upheaval in the church too. Thinkers such as Erasmus and Luther began to question the teachings of the established church, and this eventually led to a breakaway from the Catholic church and the setting up of Protestant churches—an event called the Reformation.

The set focuses on Europe, but it also looks at how societies in other parts of the world such as Africa, China, India, and the Americas were developing, and the ways in which the Islamic and Christian worlds interacted.

The entries in this set are arranged alphabetically and are illustrated with paintings, photographs, drawings, and maps, many from the Renaissance period. Each entry ends with a list of cross-references to other entries in the set, and at the end of each book there is a timeline to help you relate events to one another in time.

There is also a useful "Further Reading" list that includes websites, a glossary of special terms, and an index covering the whole set.

Contents

VOLUME 9

Religious Dissent

Above: A 15th-century book illustration showing the Catholic church as a castle being defended by monks, bishops, and the pope (center) against the attacks of heretics and unbelievers.

Religious dissent, or the refusal to accept the beliefs or practices of the established church, was widespread in Renaissance times, when the Catholic church was eager to protect its own spiritual authority. People had disagreed with the official teachings of Catholicism for centuries before the Reformation of the 16th century and the formation of the Protestant churches. Even within the new churches, however, there were dissenters who refused to follow official teachings. Like Catholic dissenters, they were persecuted for their beliefs.

In the late Middle Ages Christianity was split by bitter arguments about the nature of God and the form of worship. Whenever one view became dominant in the church, other views were condemned as heresy, or wrong belief. The church defended its spiritual authority by violence when necessary. From the late 11th to the late 13th century, for example, it launched crusades (holy wars) against Muslims in the Holy Land and against Christian dissenters within Europe, called the Albigensians and Waldensians. From the 12th century the church used inquisitors (investigators) to seek out and punish heretics.

The church saw many threats from nonbelievers in the 15th century. The Islamic Ottoman Empire had repossessed the Holy Land, controlled southeastern Europe, and captured Constantinople in 1453. In Spain there were large populations of Jews and Muslims, and Judaism remained strong in other parts of Europe. Superstition and folk belief also undermined the spiritual authority of the church.

DISSENT WITHIN CATHOLICISM

There was also widespread dissent within Christianity that reflected two often related concerns. Some people disagreed with Catholic doctrine, or spiritual teaching. They argued about the nature of God or the importance of priests in worship and wanted to return to what they saw as a purer form of religion. Other critics objected to the church's greed, corruption, and lack of spirituality. The papacy was based in

Avignon in the south of France in the late 14th century and was under the influence of the French king. Many churchmen were rich landowners, more concerned with wealth and power than with their congregations.

JOHN WYCLIFFE

Two of the most influential dissenters of the early Renaissance were the Englishman John Wycliffe and the Bohemian Jan Hus. Wycliffe (about 1329–1384) was educated at the University of Oxford, where he later taught in addition to being a parish priest. Wycliffe became increasingly critical of the church's practices and beliefs. In 1378 he set out his ideas that the true church was a body of believers who looked directly to God for their salvation, without the need for priests. They would rely on the teachings of the Bible, not the traditions of the church. He argued that, according to the Bible, the pope was not very important—nor,

for that matter, were monks and nuns. He rejected the belief that during the Mass, or Eucharist, the priest's blessing miraculously changed wine and bread into the blood and body of Christ.

The church authorities formally condemned Wycliffe's teachings in 1382. He continued to criticize the church, however, and inspired his followers to translate the Bible into English so that ordinary people could read and understand it for themselves.

Wycliffe died in 1384, but his ideas were carried forward by his supporters, known as Lollards. The Lollards had their own preachers to spread their teaching and gained many influential followers. In 1401, however, the English government passed a law condemning heretics to be burned at the stake. Many Lollards were put to death. After an unsuccessful rebellion in 1414 the Lollards were driven underground, although some of them remained active in secret.

Left: A 19th-century painting showing the English reformer John Wycliffe reading from the first English translation of the Bible, which he inspired his followers to make. Listening to the reading on the right of the picture sits John of Gaunt (1340–1399), the king's uncle and a supporter of Wycliffe.

Wycliffe's teachings also inspired the preacher Jan Hus (about 1372–1415), who lived in Bohemia, now the Czech Republic. Hus was educated at Prague University, where he later became a preacher. In his passionate sermons he criticized the church as Wycliffe had. In particular, he rejected the idea that the pope was the supreme spiritual authority. He also attacked the sale of indulgences, which were certificates sold by the church to excuse worshipers from a certain amount of time in purgatory, the realm where it was thought the dead suffered punishment for their sins. In effect, indulgences made it possible to buy forgiveness.

In 1411 Hus was excommunicated (expelled from the church). The next year he fled Prague and in exile wrote his most important work, *De Ecclesia* ("Concerning the Church"), which set out his beliefs. In 1414 Hus was summoned to a church council at Constance in Germany to defend his views. He agreed to attend only when he received a guarantee of safe conduct from Sigismund, king of Hungary and Germany. But when Hus arrived, he was imprisoned, condemned to death, and burned on July 6, 1415.

Hus became a national hero in Bohemia, and his followers, called Hussites, fought a nationalist war against Sigismund and the church. In 1436 the Council of Basel ended the war and readmitted the Hussites to the Catholic church.

SAVONAROLA

Another challenge to accepted church teaching came in Florence, in central Italy. For a few years at the end of the 15th century the Dominican prior Girolamo Savonarola (1452–1498) took advantage of political upheaval in the city to establish a virtual dictatorship. Savonarola preached the establishment of an ideal Christian state, free of corruption and worldly distractions. He found an enthusiastic following among many Florentines. His criticism of the pope, however, led to his excommunication from the

Right: An engraving from a 16th-century book of martyrs showing 13 Protestants being burned as heretics in England during the reign of Mary I (1553–1558). She was an ardent Catholic who actively persecuted Protestants because of their faith.

THOMAS MÜNZER

The German Thomas Münzer (about 1490–1525) was a leading religious and social reformer. He was first influenced by the ideas of Martin Luther, but went on to develop his own belief that people should be guided by the inner light of the Holy Spirit, rather than by the word of the Scriptures, as the Lutherans taught. He also believed that the common people would be the means of setting up God's will on earth. In 1520 he began to preach in the industrial town of Zwickau, attacking the church and demanding reforms to help the poor. After being expelled from Zwickau he traveled from town to town spreading his revolutionary ideas. He preached a revolt against the existing social order, and in 1525 he led an army of several thousand peasants to fight against injustice. Although successful at first, the peasants were eventually crushed by the troops of the duke of Saxony at the battle of Frankenhausen. Münzer was taken prisoner and was later tried and executed.

TOMAS MVNCER PREDIGER ZV ALSTET IN DVRINGEN.

Right: A 17th-century engraving of Thomas Münzer, the Protestant theologian and revolutionary who led a revolt against the existing social order in 1525.

church. When he lost some strong political allies, he was captured, tried, and burned as a heretic.

The Reformation, begun by Martin Luther in 1517, echoed earlier religious dissent. Like Hus, Luther protested the sale of indulgences; like Wycliffe, he emphasized the importance of reading the Bible. In their turn Luther and his early followers were condemned by the Catholic church as dissenters. But even after the establishment of the Protestant churches that emerged from their dissent, dissent itself continued.

THE ANABAPTISTS

The most notable of the Protestant dissenters were the Anabaptists, so named because they believed that Christians should be baptized as adults, when they were full members of the faith, rather than as infants, which was the usual practice. There were different groups of Anabaptists. Some were militant and violent, while others, such as the Swiss Brethren and Mennonites, preached nonviolence and tolerance. Most, however, rejected the authority of the church; some even rejected the authority of civil rulers, arguing that God's authority was superior. This made them many enemies. The Anabaptists were attacked by both Catholics and Protestants, and thousands were put to death in different parts of Europe. Descendants of the Anabaptists, such as the Hutterites and the Mennonites, later moved to the New World in search of religious tolerance.

SEE ALSO

♦ Biblical
  Studies
♦ Catholic
  Church
♦ Clergy
♦ Luther
♦ Papacy
♦ Protestantism
♦ Reformation
♦ Savonarola

Religious Orders

From the fourth century many Christians chose to withdraw from the everyday world and live in secluded communities to worship God. The daily routine of these monks and nuns was guided by a set of regulations called a rule, and communities bound by the same rule were known as religious orders. By the time of the Renaissance many of the old orders had come under attack for their worldliness and wealth. Some groups of monks and nuns chose to break away and form more spiritual and disciplined houses. New orders founded in the 16th century, such as the Jesuits and Capuchins, dedicated themselves to missionary work and helped renew Catholic spirituality, leading the Counter Reformation.

In the ninth century the most common rule found in monasteries was that written by Saint Benedict of Nursia (around 480–547), and the monks and

Some of the Catholic church's fiercest critics came from within the religious orders

nuns who followed it were known as Benedictines. In 1098 a devout group of Benedictine monks who were dissatisfied with the relaxed observance of their abbey broke away and formed a new order, the Cistercians.

MENDICANT ORDERS

In the 13th century the Franciscans and Dominicans were formed. They were named for their founders, Francis of Assisi and Dominic de Guzman, and were known as mendicant ("begging") orders because they relied on gifts of food and money to survive. Their members were called friars. Friars often wandered from place to place rather than living in a community. Another mendicant order was the Carmelites, named for Mount Carmel in Palestine where the order was formed. In the 13th century the Carmelites settled in Europe and by 1400 they had founded more than 150 religious houses.

Below: A 14th-century painting showing Francis of Assisi (center) giving the rule to his two orders, the Franciscans, founded in 1209, and the Poor Clares, an order for women that was founded in 1212.

SAINT TERESA OF AVILA

Teresa of Avila was an important religious reformer and mystic, famous for her visions. Born into a noble Spanish family in 1515, Teresa joined a Carmelite convent in Avila as a young woman and devoted her life to prayer. At the age of 40 she had a powerful mystical experience while praying before a statue of Christ, and from then on she experienced many visions. In order to live a stricter religious way of life, she founded her own convent with a more demanding routine in 1562.

With the help of her fellow Spanish mystic, Saint John of the Cross, Teresa reformed the Carmelite order by founding a new movement known as the Discalced ("Barefoot") Carmelites, whose members wore thin sandals instead of shoes as a sign of humility. They lived austere lives and were particularly drawn to praying and mystical experiences. At first the unreformed Carmelites were hostile to the new order. But eventually the Discalced were given official approval by the pope in 1593.

As well as being devout, Teresa was a strong, practical woman who had to battle hard to have her new order accepted. She wrote many letters, poems, and books, such as *The Way of the Perfect* and *Interior Mansions*, which describe her spiritual experiences.

Right: A 16th-century painting of Teresa of Avila writing through the inspiration of the Holy Spirit, shown as a dove.

REFORMATION AND REFORM

By the 15th century many people thought the religious orders had become lazy and worldly. This led to reform movements, often by monks and nuns who had become disillusioned with the church. Some of the Catholic church's fiercest critics came from within the religious orders: Martin Luther, the founder of Protestantism, was an Augustinian monk, and Savonarola, who railed against the pope and clergy in Florence, a Dominican friar.

Orders formed in the 16th century focused their efforts on teaching and converting. In the 1520s a branch of the Franciscans was founded in central Italy and called the Capuchins, for the *capuche* ("pointed hood") that they wore. Like the Jesuit order, founded in 1537 by Ignatius Loyola, the Capuchins were energetic missionaries, preaching the Catholic faith in Protestant countries in Europe and farther abroad. The Theatine order was also established in the 1520s (it was named for one of its founders, the bishop of Chieti, or Theate, in Italy). The Theatines' main aim was to reform the corrupt practices of the church—they owned no property and were not allowed to beg.

Between 1545 and 1563 Catholic church leaders met at the Council of Trent and recognized the importance of religious orders in the reinvigoration of Catholicism. In particular, the Jesuits became known as the spearhead of the Counter Reformation.

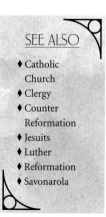

SEE ALSO

♦ Catholic Church
♦ Clergy
♦ Counter Reformation
♦ Jesuits
♦ Luther
♦ Reformation
♦ Savonarola

Religious Themes in Art

During the Renaissance most paintings and sculptures had religious themes. They showed events described in the Bible, especially the New Testament, or told stories about the life of the Virgin Mary and the saints. The most important function of such works of art was to teach or remind people about the principal beliefs of Christianity.

People living during the Renaissance were able to recognize the general subject of a religious work very quickly. Even if they were unable to read, people were familiar with the stories of the Bible and the saints. Artists showed these stories in ways that had been used by generations of painters and sculptors so that their images were easy to understand. They used long-established symbols such as a halo (a disk of light around a person's head) to indicate a saint or deep-blue robes to show the Virgin Mary.

THE LIFE OF CHRIST

The central theme of religious art was the life of Christ, based mainly on the accounts included in the gospels of the New Testament. Painters and sculptors generally portrayed the most dramatic, moving, and meaningful parts of the

gospels: Christ's birth and death. These subjects were often depicted as part of an altarpiece, a decorated structure behind an altar, so they were at the center of Catholic worship and ritual.

Christ's birth is called the Nativity. Paintings of the Nativity show the Virgin and Child in a stable, often with three shepherds, three kings (also called magi), angels, and animals. Sometimes artists included symbols that refer to Christ's Passion—the name for his death and resurrection—

Above: A painting of the Deposition (1521) by the artist known as Il Rosso Fiorentino. Rosso used harsh lighting and bright colors to add drama to the scene, which shows Christ's body being removed from the cross and the grief of his followers.

and Mary's purity. They include certain flowers like irises, lilies, columbines, and roses, as can be seen in *The Portinari Altarpiece* (see Volume 4, page 7) and *The Adoration of the Magi* by the 15th-century Flemish painter Hugo van der Goes.

Paintings and carvings of the Crucifixion, showing Christ on the cross, were often the main images used in altarpieces. They showed Christ's suffering for mankind. Artists, particularly those in northern Europe, drew attention to the pain of his sacrifice, showing blood spurting out of the wounds where nails pierced Christ's feet and hands. The 16th-century

---

Artists showed the stories of the Bible in ways that had been used by generations of painters and sculptors

---

German painter Matthias Grünewald's *Isenheim Altarpiece* (see Volume 4, page 41) is a particularly harrowing picture of Christ's bruised and battered body.

Renaissance artists also showed other stages of Christ's Passion. The Deposition (also called the Descent from the Cross) is the name given to the moment when Christ's followers took his dead body down from the cross. The Lamentation showed a similar scene in which Christ's family and followers weep over his dead body. Paintings and sculptures depicting the Deposition and Lamentation are often very emotional. In contrast, pictures of the Resurrection, when Christ rose on the third day after his death, show Jesus as triumphant and godlike as he emerges from his tomb.

THE LAST JUDGMENT

Paintings and carvings of the Last Judgment were popular in churches from the 13th century onward. They showed the moment when Christians believe that Christ will come to earth a second time to judge the souls of every human who has ever lived and will send the wicked to hell and the good to heaven. The subject was often carved over the main door to a church as well as being a popular subject for paintings. Hieronymous Bosch, Fra Angelico, and Michelangelo painted some of the best-known pictures of the Last Judgment. Artists often included terrifying images of devils torturing the damned to warn believers that they must lead good lives if they wanted to avoid such a terrible fate.

Above: A detail from a painting of the Last Judgment (1433) by Fra Angelico showing the damned being tortured in hell.

During the Middle Ages the Virgin Mary became increasingly important for many Christians. People believed that she acted as a go-between between human beings and God, and so they turned to her in times of need. Most homes had a small image of the Virgin, also called the Madonna (Italian for "My Lady"). In Italy there was even a special kind of painter called a *madonniero* who specialized in making images of the Virgin.

THE LIFE OF THE VIRGIN

The most common image of the Virgin showed her with the Christ child. In the Middle Ages such images were usually very stylized (artificial looking) and were copies of earlier pictures of the subject. From the 15th century, however, artists portrayed the Virgin and Child in a more lifelike way, so that Mary appeared almost like an ordinary mother with her child. Paintings of the Madonna by Raphael and Giovanni Bellini, for example, emphasize her humanity and kindness.

Other pictures of the Virgin show her grief at her son's death. In the kind of painting and sculpture known as a pietà (Italian for "pity"), the Virgin supports the dead Christ in her lap. Painters and sculptors also showed other scenes from the life of the Virgin. The most popular of these scenes was the Annunciation, when the angel Gabriel announces to Mary that God has chosen her to be the mother of Christ. Some of the best-known

From the 15th century artists portrayed the Virgin and Child in a more lifelike way

paintings of the subject were by Fra Angelico (see Volume 1, page 24), Botticelli, and Leonardo da Vinci.

The gospels do not provide much information about the Virgin, and over the centuries many legends grew up about her life. In the 15th century the Catholic church adopted some of these stories as doctrines (beliefs), including the doctrine of the Assumption: the belief that Mary, like Christ, was resurrected after her death and rose to heaven. The Assumption became a popular theme in 16th-century art.

*Above: Leonardo da Vinci's painting **The Annunciation** (about 1472–1475). The Virgin Mary is shown weaving and raising her left hand in surprise as she sees the angel Gabriel. Gabriel kneels in respect and raises his right hand as he tells Mary that she will be the mother of Christ. In his left hand Gabriel holds a lily, a flower that symbolizes Mary's purity.*

SAINTS AND SYMBOLS

Churches were often dedicated to particular saints and contained paintings and sculptures in their honor. Religious orders such as the Franciscans commemorated the life of their founding saints in altarpieces or frescoes (wall paintings). Individual patrons (the people who ordered and paid for pictures and sculptures) often also had a favorite saint whom they wanted shown in the works of art they ordered. Some saints were thought to help people in particular circumstances. For example, people called on Saint Sebastian to protect them from the plague.

Artists showed saints with their traditional attributes, or symbols, so that they could be instantly recognized. Saint John the Baptist was shown wearing rags and carrying a staff; Mary Magdalene was shown with the pot of ointment with which she had bathed Christ's feet; Saint Peter was shown holding the key to heaven; and Saint Jerome was shown with a cardinal's hat and a lion. The attributes of some saints referred to the way that they had been tortured or put to death for their Christian beliefs. Saint Catherine was shown with a wheel because she had been tortured on a machine made from four spiked wheels, while Saint Sebastian was shown pierced by arrows because he had been shot with arrows.

Since many saints had lived centuries before the Renaissance, artists often relied on tradition and legend for information about their lives. The most important source of information for artists was a 13th-century collection of stories called *The Golden Legend*.

Right: This 15th-century Italian painting shows Saint Catherine with her traditional symbol, a spiked wheel. She is also shown holding a sword because she was beheaded after being tortured.

Paintings and sculptures with religious themes remained the most widely produced works of art throughout the 15th and 16th centuries. They were made in great numbers for churches, cathedrals, and also for people's homes.

CHANGING ATTITUDES

The Protestant religion that emerged at the beginning of the 16th century placed more emphasis on the word of the Bible rather than pictures and sculptures illustrating it. Protestant churches and worship were much plainer than Catholic ones and contained far fewer works of art.

In response to the Protestant challenge the Catholic church also introduced stricter guidelines for artists at a meeting of senior churchmen called the Council of Trent. The council discussed many subjects, including the place of art in worship. It specified which subjects artists could show—those not actually described in the Bible were discouraged—and also how they should be portrayed. Nude (unclothed) figures were discouraged, and the council instructed that draperies (clothes) should be painted over the nudes in Michelangelo's painting of the Last Judgment (1534–1541) in the Sistine Chapel.

SEE ALSO

♦ Angelico, Fra
♦ Bellini, Giovanni
♦ Biblical Studies
♦ Bosch
♦ Catholic Church
♦ Counter Reformation
♦ German Art
♦ Giotto
♦ Leonardo da Vinci
♦ Michelangelo
♦ Naturalism
♦ Painting

Renaissance, Idea of

The term "Renaissance" is French for "rebirth." It is used to describe a period of cultural change that took place during the 15th and 16th centuries, when painters, sculptors, and scholars became interested in reviving classical (ancient Greek and Roman) culture. The trend began in Italy, with which the Renaissance is most closely associated, before spreading to other European countries. Historians also use the term "Renaissance" in a more general sense to describe advances in thinking, science, exploration, society, and government that also took place.

The Swiss scholar Jacob Burckhardt (1818–1897) first popularized the use of the word "Renaissance" that is familiar today. In a book called *The Civilization of the Renaissance in Italy* (1860) he applied the term to the rebirth of classical culture that took place in Italy in the 15th and 16th centuries. He argued, further, that the Italian civilization of this period had largely shaped the European culture and society of his own time.

EARLY IDEAS OF A NEW AGE
Burckhardt's ideas about an Italian renaissance were not entirely new. In fact, many Italian artists, writers, and scholars of the 15th and 16th centuries had themselves felt that they belonged to a new age. They not only believed that they were reviving and rivaling the achievements of ancient Greece and Rome, but that they were overturning the ignorance of preceding centuries.

They came to call this earlier age the "Middle Ages," the time between the classical and modern ages.

In the 14th century the poet and scholar Petrarch, for example, had already looked forward to a rebirth of classical art after what he termed the "darkness" that followed the decline of the western Roman Empire. By the 15th and 16th centuries many people believed that Petrarch's hopes had been fulfilled. The 15th-century architect and writer Leon Battista Alberti said that some of his fellow artists—like the architect Brunelleschi, the sculptor Donatello, and the painter Masaccio—were the equal of classical artists.

Below: A painting showing artists studying the works of Michelangelo by the 17th-century Italian painter Nicodemo Ferrucci. Many people, including the 16th-century painter and art historian Giorgio Vasari, saw Michelangelo's art as the peak of Renaissance achievements.

The most important source for Burckhardt's ideas about the Italian Renaissance, however, was the 16th-century artist and critic Giorgio Vasari (1511–1574). In his book *Lives of the Artists* (1550) he argued that the arts had first reached a peak in ancient Rome, had died with the decline of the Roman Empire, and had been revived in the 14th century by the Florentine painter Giotto. He wrote that it was only in his own lifetime, particularly in the work of Leonardo da Vinci, Raphael, and Michelangelo, that the arts had become truly great again. Vasari used the term *rinascita* (Italian for "rebirth") to describe this revival.

OBJECTIONS TO THE TERM

Burckhardt's ideas on the Renaissance gained wide acceptance and still shape current thinking about the period. However, some scholars have criticized his views. Their main objection is that Burckhardt's idea of the Renaissance encourages people to think that at the beginning of the 15th century there was a sudden break with the culture of the Middle Ages. Most scholars today argue that any changes that took place were in fact gradual and had already begun in the Middle Ages. They also point out that the 15th and 16th centuries were a time not only of great artistic and cultural advance, but also of ignorance, superstition, violence, and corruption. Indeed, life for the poorer members of society continued much as it had for centuries.

A MISLEADING VIEW OF ART

Similarly, art historians criticize Vasari's views about an artistic revival because such ideas discount the achievements of medieval artists. His notion of progress in the arts can also lead people to assume that art created

after the 16th century could only decline, since perfection cannot be improved upon. Critics point out that Vasari's emphasis on the role of artists from Florence and Rome has led people to ignore the work of artists from other regions of Italy as well as from the rest of Europe—not to mention those not working in the "up-to-date" style that he admired.

USING THE TERM TODAY

Despite these shortcomings, however, the term "Renaissance" can still be useful today. It is helpful as a label to describe a period in which the revival of classical values by scholars, artists, and rulers became widespread and fashionable. But it should be remembered that a new chapter of history did not suddenly begin and that the preceding Middle Ages had been in many ways an equally significant period of cultural achievement.

Above: A picture of Raphael in his studio, painted by the 19th-century artist Ingres.

Rome

Although Rome had once flourished as the heart of a huge empire, its importance declined during the Middle Ages, and most of its buildings fell into ruin. From the 15th century the Renaissance popes spent large sums of money rebuilding Rome to emphasize its position as the center of the Catholic church. It gained in political importance and became a leading center of art, architecture, and culture.

Ancient Rome was famous for its great public buildings, broad squares, and paved streets, and as the center of the greatest empire Europe had ever known. At its height in the second century A.D. the city was home to more than a million people. The medieval city, by contrast, was dirty, chaotic, and disease-ridden. Most of the ancient buildings lay in ruins, and about three-quarters of the city had been abandoned or turned into farmland.

Long after the collapse of the Roman Empire in western Europe, however, people continued to think of Rome as a symbol of civilization—of peace, order, and artistic excellence. The city was also revered as the center of the Christian world. Since early times Rome had been the seat of the bishop of Rome—known as the pope—who was widely held to be the leader of the Christian church. Over the centuries the popes came to rule Rome much as if they were its kings.

A CITY IN DECLINE

In 800 A.D. the pope crowned the Frankish king Charlemagne "Emperor of the West" in the church of Saint Peter's. In theory Rome was the capital

Above: **The Tiber River at Castel Sant'Angelo** *by the Dutch painter Gaspare van Wittel (1653–1736). Wittel specialized in painting views of Rome, and this picture shows the city much as it would have looked at the end of the Renaissance. The recently completed church of Saint Peter's can be seen in the center, and the heavily fortified Castel Sant'Angelo is shown at right.*

city of Charlemagne's new Christian empire. In reality, however, the Holy Roman Empire, as it became known, was never based in Rome or even in Italy. Its main territories lay far to the north, in Germany. The Holy Roman emperors granted the popes control over the city of Rome and the lands of central Italy, called the Papal States.

Although many Italian cities began to flourish from the 10th century onward, Rome remained backward and poor, with very little industry. In the mid-14th century its population was just 17,000, and most Romans lived in slums. What income the city enjoyed came from the pilgrims who visited its holy sites, the most important of which was the church of Saint Peter's.

The popes often found it difficult to control Rome, as great landowning families struggled for power. In 1309 the popes were forced to abandon the city altogether and moved to Avignon in southern France. In their absence the city fell into anarchy. Around 1400 one visitor to Rome described it as a city filled with huts, thieves, and rats.

REVIVAL AND RENAISSANCE
In 1420 Pope Martin V returned the papacy to Rome. He brought peace and order to the city and set up a new government with sweeping powers. Slowly the city revived. Under Martin's successors, notably Nicholas V and Sixtus IV, the streets were paved, and grand new buildings were constructed.

THE SACK OF ROME

On May 5, 1527, the largely Protestant troops of the Holy Roman emperor Charles V swarmed into Rome. The soldiers went on a week-long rampage, killing many of the city's inhabitants and plundering its treasures. Thousands of houses and hundreds of churches and palaces were destroyed, as were many masterpieces of ancient and Renaissance art. Pope Clement VII took refuge in the ancient Roman fortress of Castel Sant'Angelo, where he was defended for seven months by his bodyguard of Swiss soldiers before being forced to flee Rome in disguise. Meanwhile the invaders occupied the Vatican. They used precious ancient manuscripts as bedding for their horses and scratched graffiti on the frescoes (wall paintings). The emperor's troops finally left Rome in December, when an outbreak of plague made the city unsafe.

Above: An engraving by the 17th-century German printmaker Mathäus Merian showing the sack of Rome. Charles V's soldiers are mocking the pope by dressing up and imitating a papal procession.

By the end of the 15th century the papal court was one of the most important in Europe. Rome bristled with building projects, as cardinals (leading churchmen) competed with one another to build the finest palaces. Diplomats flocked to the city from all over Europe. Rome became notorious for the luxurious, extravagant lifestyle of some of its inhabitants.

Under Pope Julius II (pope 1503–1513) Rome replaced Florence as the center of Renaissance culture. Julius employed Donato Bramante to rebuild Saint Peter's and summoned some of the greatest artists of the age, including Michelangelo and Raphael, to decorate Rome's churches and palaces.

DISCONTENT AND DISASTER

When Julius died his successor, Pope Leo X, continued to order many new buildings and works of art to glorify the city. However, many Catholics in other parts of Europe thought the popes were too extravagant in their spending and objected to the way that they raised money. In 1517 the German monk Martin Luther wrote down his objections in a document called the 95 theses (articles), which marked the start of the religious movement known as the Reformation.

In 1527 disaster struck Rome. As the army of the Holy Roman emperor Charles V swept down through Italy, it sacked the almost defenseless city (see box on page 17). The triumphant emperor forced the pope to crown him emperor. In return, however, he recognized the pope as the rightful ruler of Rome.

A REFORMED ROME

The catastrophe left the popes determined to transform Rome into a unified, well-ordered city. The task was made all the more urgent by the rapid rise of Protestantism in northern Europe. The papacy wanted to show that Rome was the fitting and rightful center of the Christian world.

Under 16th-century popes like Pius IV and Sixtus V Rome started to become the imposing city it is today. Architects carved out grand new thoroughfares that connected different parts of the city and built spacious new piazzas, or squares, in which thousands of pilgrims could gather. New housing was developed, and the city's water supply was improved. In rebuilding Rome, however, the popes took little care to preserve the city's ancient remains, many of which were used as sources of building material.

Above: A painting by Gaspare van Wittel showing the Piazza del Popolo. The piazza was laid out in the mid-16th century on the city outskirts. Pope Sixtus V built new streets linking it to the city center and put up the obelisk.

SEE ALSO

- Antiquities
- Baroque
- Borgia Family
- Bramante
- Catholic Church
- Charles V
- Classicism
- Holy Roman Empire
- Leo X
- Luther
- Martin V
- Michelangelo
- Papacy
- Papal States
- Raphael
- Saint Peter's, Rome
- Vatican

Russia

Russia is a vast land at the eastern edge of Europe, crossed by mighty rivers such as the Don and the Volga. From the 13th to the 15th century the region was divided into rival states, all of which paid tribute to Mongol overlords. One Russian principality, Moscow, or Muscovy, gradually absorbed the rest, defied the Mongols, and under Ivan III and Ivan the Terrible expanded eastward. But the new Muscovy was still backward and unstable, and during the so-called Time of Troubles at the beginning of the 17th century its very survival was threatened.

In the early Middle Ages the main center of Russian culture was around Kiev, to the north of the Black Sea. Russians gradually spread out far to the east and northeast, occupying large areas of tundra (subarctic regions of marshy plain), forests, and steppes (dry plains). In the years 1237 to 1240 the various Russian principalities were defeated by the Mongol armies that were conquering large parts of Asia and Europe. The Russian princes made peace with the Mongols and were allowed to continue governing their realms as long as they paid regular tribute (taxes) to their conquerors.

THE GOLDEN HORDE

This was the situation when the gigantic Mongol Empire broke up into separate states known as khanates. The khanate of the Golden Horde was the westernmost branch of the Mongol peoples, whom the Russians called Tartars. It dominated the Russian lands from bases to the east along the Volga, and to the south in the Crimea. The

Above: A 20th-century Russian painting depicting the Russian troops on the morning of the battle of Kulikovo, fought between the Russians and the Golden Horde in 1380. Under the leadership of Prince Dmitry Donskoi the Russian forces won a resounding victory over the previously invincible Mongols.

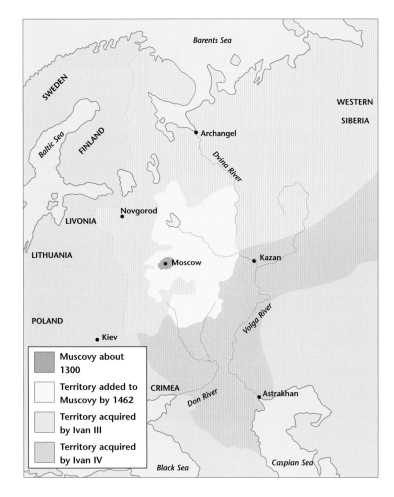

Above: A map showing the expansion of Muscovy from 1300 to the death of Ivan the Terrible in 1584.

prince of Muscovy to challenge the Golden Horde, winning a great victory at Kulikovo in 1380. It was not enough to end the domination of Russia by the Tartars, but it demonstrated that the Mongols were no longer invincible.

A DETERMINED PRINCE

The struggle went on intermittently until 1462, when Ivan III (ruled 1462–1505) became grand prince of Muscovy. Like Ivan Kalita, he combined caution with determination. Three of the four remaining princely states were soon under his control, but the large and wealthy Russian republic of Novgorod, in the far north, proved harder to subdue. Finally, after two wars, Novgorod was annexed in 1478, and its loyalty assured by deporting the hostile upper classes to central Russia.

Meanwhile Ivan ignored demands from the Golden Horde to pay tribute, and in 1480 the Tartars finally decided to attack. To the south the Crimea was now a separate khanate, allied with Muscovy. But the horde had a powerful ally in Lithuania, a large European state to the west of Muscovy. The final showdown was an anticlimax. The Russian and Tartar armies came face to face, each lining a bank of the Ugra River. After a standoff lasting several weeks both withdrew—the Tartars disconcerted by the nonarrival of the Lithuanians, the Russians fearful of a Lithuanian attack from behind that never came. But Tartar claims to overlordship had been disposed of once and for all.

REBELLIOUS BROTHERS

The crisis of 1480 was complicated by the rebellion of Ivan's own brothers, who were angered by his policy of whittling away the powers and privileges of other members of the

Russians remained subject to the Golden Horde for over two centuries, during which time Muscovy grew in importance. Its chief city, Moscow, lay at the heart of Russia's transportation and river systems. It was well placed to expand, but its rise also owed much to a series of shrewd princes.

Among them was Ivan I, nicknamed Kalita ("Moneybags"), who ruled from 1328 to 1340. His policy was to work with the Tartars, winning their trust and collecting tribute for them from his fellow Russians. Ivan became wealthy and was able to buy new territories for Muscovy. He took the title of grand prince, implying he was superior to the other Russian princes.

While Ivan and his successors grew stronger, Tartar power began to decline. Dmitry Donskoi was the first

EARLY RUSSIA

The Russians and other Slavic peoples settled in eastern Europe from the sixth century A.D. The first Russian state was created by the Vikings, known as Varangians, who invaded from the north and founded the kingdom of Kiev Rus in the ninth century. Warfare and trade led to contacts between Kiev Rus and the Greek empire of Byzantium, and under Byzantine influence the Russians were converted to Orthodox Christianity. While the Russians spread far to the east and north, Kiev Rus broke up into a number of rival principalities, which were conquered in 1237–1240 by the Tartars. One of Russia's great heroes, Prince Alexander Nevsky, fought off western invaders from Sweden and the region of the Teutonic Knights on the Baltic coast. But he agreed to pay tribute to the Mongols, and Tartar overlordship lasted for centuries.

ruling family. Though he was forced to compromise in 1480, Ivan pursued his policy even more ruthlessly once the crisis was past. By the time of his death in 1505 he was supreme within Muscovy, and Muscovy was the supreme Russian state.

IMPERIAL AMBITIONS

Ivan tried to give his rule a special religious and imperial authority. In 1453 the Byzantine Empire was destroyed by the Ottoman Turks. Ivan presented himself as the natural successor to the Byzantine emperors. In 1472 he married the last emperor's niece, Sophia, and adopted the Byzantine double-headed eagle as his own imperial symbol. He also sometimes used the titles czar (the Russian equivalent of "Caesar" or emperor) and autocrat (absolute ruler). His authority was further strengthened by the backing of the Orthodox church and by the belief that Moscow was now the center of the church, and therefore of culture, in succession to ancient Rome and Byzantine Constantinople.

But family problems and the ambitions of the great nobles—the boyars—undermined Ivan's authority. Disputes over the succession to his throne darkened his last years. He was succeeded by his son, Vasily.

In 1533, following a period of stability, a three-year-old child became grand prince as Ivan IV. Dominated by noble families and their feuds, the young Ivan experienced dangers and

Left: Czar Ivan "the Terrible," as depicted in a 19th-century Russian painting. Ivan, who ruled from 1533 to 1584, brought many benefits to Russia— he reformed the legal code and the administrative systems of the country and also extended and strengthened the Russian state. But continuous wars drained resources, and Ivan's unpredictable behavior in later life ushered in a reign of terror.

humiliations during his childhood that left him with a permanent distrust of the boyars.

THE FIRST CZAR

When he was 16, Ivan had himself crowned czar. He was the first Russian ruler to make it his official title, claiming to be an all-powerful autocrat answerable only to God. He reigned moderately for some years, and from 1552 to 1556 he won the greatest success of his reign, destroying the Tartar khanates of Kazan and Astrakhan. Muscovy now commanded the entire region surrounding the Volga River, opening the way for the expeditions that in time conquered western Siberia and began Russian colonization across Asia.

To improve trade, Muscovy needed better contacts with Europe. In 1553 the English navigator Richard Chancellor reached Moscow by sailing over the top of Scandinavia and down the Dvina River. Useful trade contacts with Elizabethan England followed, but the route was a long and hazardous one. Recognizing that Muscovy needed a more direct outlet to Europe, Ivan began a series of wars against the Swedes, Poles, and Lithuanians, hoping to seize the Baltic province of Livonia (present-day Latvia).

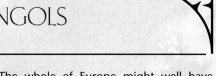

THE MONGOLS

The Mongols were a group of nomadic tribes who originally lived in northeast Asia. They were united in 1206 by Temujin, a chief who was proclaimed Genghis Khan, or "Lord of the Earth." Under his leadership the Mongols' horsemanship, discipline, and terrible cruelty made them invincible. Genghis Khan and his successors conquered a vast Asian empire, subdued the Russians, and overcame armies in Poland and Hungary.

The whole of Europe might well have been conquered if the Mongol forces had not been recalled when a new great khan had to be elected. In 1260 the fourth great khan, Kublai, became emperor of China. By that time the Mongol Empire was starting to split up into independent khanates; but the Mongols remained formidable for centuries more, founding new states, including the great Mogul Empire in India.

Left: A 14th-century Persian illustration of Mongol warriors. In the Middle Ages the Mongol forces were feared throughout Asia, and they conquered many of the Russian principalities.

RUSSIAN ART

From the time that the grand prince of Kiev adopted Byzantine Christianity in the 10th century, Russian art was dominated by the influence of the Byzantine, or Orthodox, church. Russian artists specialized in painting icons—pictures of saints or other holy people that were usually done on a wooden panel. The most celebrated of all Russian icon painters was Andrey Rublyov (about 1360–1430). He trained as an assistant to Theophanes the Greek (about 1370–1405), who was a Byzantine painter working in Russia. Rublyov probably helped paint some of the icons in the Cathedral of the Annunciation in the Kremlin.

After the fall of Constantinople in 1453 Moscow became a center of Orthodox Christianity. Architects from Italy were commissioned to build monumental buildings in Moscow that would reflect its new importance. The multidomed Cathedral of Saint Michael (1505–1509), built by the Italian architect Alevisio Novi, shows Renaissance touches but is still essentially in the Byzantine tradition that is typical of Russian architecture. The spectacular Cathedral of Saint Basil (1554–1560) in Moscow's Red Square is purely Russian and was to influence Russian architecture for more than 100 years.

Above: An icon by Andrey Rublyov entitled The Holy Trinity. *Icons like this one were often regarded as holy objects.*

The wars lasted until 1582. They exhausted the country and ended in failure. Things were made worse by Ivan's cruel and near-insane behavior, which led to him being called "the Terrible." The first crisis was triggered by disagreements with the boyars and, in 1564, the treachery of Ivan's friend and principal commander, Prince Andrey Kurbski. In a dramatic gesture Ivan gave up the throne and left Moscow, returning only when begged to do so by the people. Then, bizarrely, he divided his realm into two, creating a large personal domain run by a kind of secret police. In both parts of Muscovy Ivan and his police conducted savage purges in which anyone suspected of disloyalty was tortured and executed or exiled. In 1570, when the czar's suspicions fell on once-independent Novgorod, the city was sacked and thousands massacred.

A measure of stability was restored, but Ivan remained unpredictable. In 1582, in a fit of rage, he killed his son and heir. The consequences were serious. After Ivan's death in 1584 his feebleminded son Fyodor became czar of a ravaged Muscovy.

BORIS GODUNOV

A forceful regent, Boris Godunov, held real power and himself became czar after Fyodor's death in 1598. Before Boris died in 1605, Muscovy had entered its "Time of Troubles," when peasant revolts and foreign invasions brought the state to the brink of destruction. The troubles ended only in 1613, when Michael Romanov was chosen as czar, founding a dynasty that ruled until 1917. Muscovy officially became "Russia" only in the early 18th century, when it emerged as a great power in Europe.

SEE ALSO
♦ Constantinople
♦ Eastern Europe
♦ Elizabeth I
♦ Orthodox Church
♦ Ottoman Empire

Saint Peter's, Rome

Saint Peter's in Rome is the most important Roman Catholic church in the world. It is built near the spot where church tradition held that Saint Peter, the leader of Christ's apostles, was buried. Constantine, who was the first Christian emperor of Rome, built an enormous church on the site in the fourth century A.D. However, by the 16th century it was in a poor state of repair. The Renaissance popes replaced Constantine's church with a grand new building, which became one of the main artistic projects of the 16th century.

Pope Julius II made the decision to demolish Constantine's church and build a new one in its place, and he himself laid the foundation stone of the new Saint Peter's on April 18, 1506. He entrusted the design of the building to Donato Bramante, the most renowned architect of the time.

The new Saint Peter's was intended to be the greatest church ever built—huge in size and magnificent in decoration. The pope wanted to emphasize the importance of Rome as the center of the Catholic church and also to assert papal authority—Saint Peter was regarded as the first pope.

BRAMANTE'S DESIGN
Bramante designed a Greek-cross church—that is, a church laid out as a cross with four arms of equal length—topped by a huge central dome. It was a massive undertaking, and by the time of Bramante's death in 1514 only a few of the foundations had been built, including those for the huge piers that were to support the dome. Bramante left no precise plans, and later architects who worked on Saint Peter's had different views about how the building should be completed. But they all retained the basic idea of a mighty dome and spent much time figuring out how to build it.

In 1527 work came to an abrupt halt when Rome was captured and looted by troops of the Holy Roman emperor Charles V. Pope Paul III revived the momentum of the project in the 1530s,

Below: Saint Peter's as it appears today. The dome is based on Michelangelo's design, while the façade, or main front, was designed by Carlo Maderna in the 17th century. The square and colonnades (seen on the right) were also created in the 17th century by Bernini.

entrusting it to the architect Antonio da Sangallo the Younger. He died in 1546, and Michelangelo then took up the role of architect of Saint Peter's.

MICHELANGELO'S ROLE

Although Michelangelo was 71 when he took over, he still had immense energy, and the building progressed more quickly than it had for many years. He pulled down some of the work of his predecessors in order to increase the power and grandeur of the design. Although he died in 1564, before the building was complete, his ideas largely determined the final appearance of Saint Peter's. The great dome was finished between 1585 and 1590, slightly steeper in shape than Michelangelo had planned.

At the beginning of the 17th century the architect Carlo Maderna added a nave (large hall) to the original Greek-cross plan to satisfy the clergy, who wanted a space for their processions. Maderna then designed the façade (main front) of the building and much of the inside. By 1612 Saint Peter's was essentially complete, and it was consecrated (dedicated to Christian worship) on November 18, 1626.

Left: A painting by the Italian artist Passignano (1558–1638) showing Michelangelo presenting a model of Saint Peter's to Pope Paul IV. Architects often made models of their designs so that their patrons (the people they were working for) could see what the finished building would look like.

The lavish decoration of the inside of the church continued throughout the 17th century, much of it created by the artist Gianlorenzo Bernini. Bernini also designed the last major addition to the outside: the colonnades (roofed structures supported by rows of columns) that enclose the large square in front of Saint Peter's.

RAISING THE MONEY

To raise money for the rebuilding of Saint Peter's, Pope Julius II appealed to monarchs and nobles throughout Europe and also promoted the sale of grants called indulgences. Catholics believed that after death their souls would spend time in purgatory, where they would be purified by suffering before they were fit to enter heaven. Buying an indulgence was supposed to reduce the amount of time that the purchaser would have to spend in purgatory. Many people disagreed with indulgences because they encouraged the belief that people could buy their way out of the consequences of sin. The most outspoken opponent was the German monk Martin Luther, who in 1517 made a public attack on the abuse of papal power. His stand ultimately led to a split in the Christian church and the development of Protestantism.

Savonarola

In Florence in central Italy in the 1480s a monk called Girolamo Savonarola (1452–1498) began to attract attention with his fiery sermons. Savonarola attacked the corruption of the ruling Medici family and the immoral lifestyle of the citizens of Renaissance Florence. He made prophecies, the most alarming of which was that Florence would be destroyed unless the citizens mended their ways. When the Medici were driven out of Florence by the French king Charles VIII, Savonarola seized the opportunity to become Florence's spiritual ruler. For four years the pleasure-seeking Renaissance city became a model of Christian virtue.

Savonarola was born into a noble family in Ferrara. Even as a young man he was deeply struck by the corrupt lifestyle of wealthy Renaissance princes and the clergy. At the age of 22 he joined the Dominican order and threw himself enthusiastically into a life of prayer and deprivation.

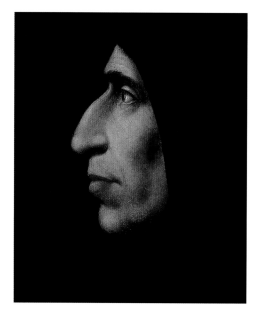

Left: A portrait of Savonarola by Fra Bartolommeo (1472–1517). Although a monk, Savonarola became the virtual ruler of Florence for a while. However, his powerful enemies in the city joined with the duke of Milan and the pope to bring him down.

In 1481 Savonarola was sent to preach in Florence, but he made little impression at first. However, following a revelation, he started to make prophecies (predictions) in his sermons. Some of these prophecies, such as the date when Pope Innocent VIII would die, came true. After traveling through Italy preaching in other cities, Savonarola returned to

SAVONAROLA AND LORENZO DE MEDICI

When Savonarola became prior of the San Marco monastery in Florence in 1491, he pointedly failed to visit the monastery's benefactor, Lorenzo de Medici. Savonarola considered Lorenzo to be a tyrant and his court one of the worst examples of decadent luxury. "Tell Lorenzo to do penance for his sins," he proclaimed, "for God will punish him and his." And Savonarola also made a prophecy that Lorenzo would die within a year. Indeed, Lorenzo did die in 1492—possibly as a result of a remedy he was taking made from powdered pearls. Before he died, Lorenzo sent for Savonarola to absolve his sins. According to legend, the preacher agreed, but only on the condition that Lorenzo restore the city's political liberties. Lorenzo refused to do this and so died without Savonarola's blessing.

Florence in 1489. By this time he was obsessed with the idea that a great calamity would visit Florence to cleanse the city of its sins.

In 1491 Savonarola became prior of the San Marco monastery in Florence and immediately set about reforming it. The monastic rule was rigidly enforced, and Savonarola set an example by wearing a habit (hooded robe) made from coarse cloth and living in a tiny cell. The number of monks in the monastery increased from 50 to 238 and included members of the city's wealthiest families.

Savonarola was now a powerful and persuasive preacher, and the Florentine citizens flocked to hear him. From the pulpit he attacked the ruler of Florence, Lorenzo de Medici, for his tyranny, his extravagance, and his patronage of pagan art. Savonarola particularly hated paintings that were supposedly religious but showed human bodies that were attractive to look at.

In 1492 Lorenzo de Medici died and was succeeded by his son Piero. When the French king Charles VIII invaded Italy in 1494, Piero handed over much of his land, including the city of Pisa. This triggered a revolution against Piero, and Savonarola took control of Florence with Charles' support. Savonarola declared that Christ now ruled the city.

SAVONAROLA'S FLORENCE

From 1494 to 1498 Savonarola's influence transformed the city. A form of democratic government was set up based on what Savonarola said was the law of Christ. Bands of Savonarola's supporters badgered people to stop gambling and wearing jewelry and frivolous clothes. At first the Florentines were enthusiastic about Savonarola's spiritual revolution. They

flocked to hand over their possessions, including ornaments, playing cards, gaming tables, and pictures of beautiful women. These items were then burned publicly in the city square in what was called a "bonfire of vanities."

Savonarola continued to preach, denouncing the corruption of the pope, Alexander VI, and the curia (papal government). Alexander banned him from preaching, an order that Savonarola ignored. This led to his excommunication (banishment from the church) in 1497.

Meanwhile, Savonarola was losing support in Florence. He was challenged to prove his holiness in an ordeal by fire. One of his supporters took up the challenge. Two great piles of fuel were prepared in a public square, each 120 ft (36m) long, with 3 ft (1m) between them. The two contestants were to run through the blazing heap—if one survived, it would prove the rightness of his cause. But at the last minute the ordeal was called off because of rain. The citizens attacked the monastery of San Marco and captured Savonarola. He was tried, tortured, and condemned to death. On May 23, 1498, he was hanged and his body burned.

Above: This 16th-century woodcut shows Savonarola preaching to an eager congregation. His impassioned sermons attracted a large following, and after his death some people worshiped him as a saint.

SEE ALSO

- Alexander VI
- Catholic Church
- City-States
- Clergy
- Florence
- France
- Italy
- Medici Family
- Papacy
- Religious Orders

Scandinavia

Following centuries of wars and shifting alliances, the Scandinavian kingdoms of Denmark, Norway, and Sweden joined together under a single Danish ruler in 1397. The fragile union lasted for 126 years but fell apart in 1523, when a young Swedish nobleman, Gustavus Vasa, led a successful Swedish revolt. It began a struggle for supremacy in the Baltic between Sweden and Denmark that went on for almost two centuries. Meanwhile, Norway remained in the union and continued to be ruled by its more powerful neighbor, Denmark.

The peoples of Denmark, Norway, and Sweden are closely related in culture and language. In their early history as Viking warriors they raided, traded, and settled in many parts of Europe. In most places they were eventually absorbed by local peoples, but their distinctive "Nordic" character survived not only in the three kingdoms but also in the Orkney and Shetland Islands north of Scotland, in Iceland, and in the Faeroe Islands, all of which belonged to Norway. Still farther west, Norwegian settlements in Greenland declined as the climate became harsher, and by the 15th century they no longer existed. At the other, eastern end of this northern world the non-Nordic people of Finland were ruled by Sweden from the 13th century.

DENMARK DOMINATES

Denmark was the strongest of the Scandinavian kingdoms from the later 14th century, mainly thanks to the

Left: A portrait of King Gustavus I, who ruled Sweden from 1523 to 1560. Gustavus secured independence for Sweden and immediately set about strengthening the country and its monarchy. By the time of his death he was an immensely rich and powerful man, as can be seen from this portrait. It was painted in 1558 and shows Gustavus dressed in sumptuous black velvet clothes patterned with gold.

achievements of King Waldemar IV (ruled 1340–1375), who fought off foreign rulers to unite his kingdom in 1361. In the 14th century Danish lands included present-day southern Sweden, giving Denmark complete control of the entrance to the Baltic Sea—the Danish Sound. Denmark was also more accessible to people and ideas from mainland Europe than its northern neighbors. But the greatest economic power in the region was the Hanseatic League of German trading towns (also called the Hansa), which controlled the lucrative Baltic trade in grain, minerals, fur, and naval supplies. The league had even managed to defeat King Waldemar in 1370, forcing him to allow their merchants freedom to trade as they pleased in Denmark. German Hansa merchants were the most powerful men in many Scandinavian towns at this time, dominating local politics through the town councils. Though gradually declining, the league remained a force in the trading towns of the Baltic for another 150 years.

UNITING THE THREE KINGDOMS

Waldemar's able daughter, Queen Margaret of Denmark, successively became regent of Denmark, Norway, and Sweden. She strengthened the power of the crown in all three countries and in 1397 drew up the Union of Kalmar, a document that committed them to be ruled by a single monarch. The union enabled her great-nephew, Eric of Pomerania, to become king, but real power rested with Margaret until her death in 1412.

Denmark benefited most from the union, becoming the center of government for all the kingdoms. Norway, ruled by Margaret from 1380, remained under Danish monarchs until 1814. However, the interests of Denmark and Sweden proved almost impossible to reconcile. After Margaret's death the less skillful Eric of Pomerania engaged in disputes with the Hansa that damaged Sweden's iron industry, sparking a successful Swedish revolt.

By 1439 Eric had been deposed in all three of his realms, and a new king, Christopher of Bavaria, managed to restore the union. However, when the Dane Christian I succeeded him in 1448, a group of Swedish nobles chose one of their own, Karl Knutsson, to rule them as Charles VIII, hoping that

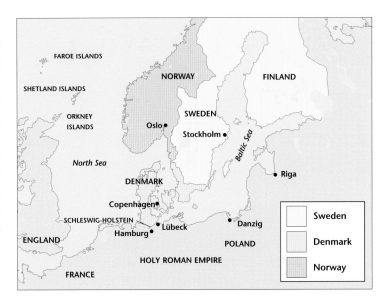

he would create a strong national monarchy. Some of the nobility preferred to remain in the union, and the situation became bewilderingly unstable—over the years Charles VIII and Christian I were alternately recognized and deposed by noble factions. By the time Charles VIII died in 1470, he had been king of Sweden three times and deposed twice.

In Denmark Christian founded the dynasty of Oldenburg, which ruled

Above: A map showing the extent of the Scandinavian kingdoms, Norway, Denmark, and Sweden, in the 15th and 16th centuries.

SOVEREIGN LADY

Queen Margaret, who brought about the Union of Kalmar, was the daughter of one of Denmark's greatest kings, Waldemar IV, and the wife of the Danish monarch Haakon VI. Waldemar died in 1375 and Haakon in 1380, making Haakon's son by Margaret, Olaf, king of both Denmark and Norway. Because Olaf was a child, Margaret became regent on his behalf. Then, in 1386 the Swedish nobility asked Margaret to help them oust their German king, Albert of Mecklenberg. Margaret's forces were victorious, and the Riksdag (the Swedish assembly) elected her "Sovereign Lady and Ruler." Margaret's position was secure, but Olaf's death in 1387 left the future of the three kingdoms uncertain. To maintain their unity, she persuaded the kingdoms to accept her sister's grandson, Eric of Pomerania, as king and to recognize the Union of Kalmar.

until 1863. During his reign the Danish crown acquired two long-disputed southern provinces, Schleswig and Holstein. To pay off the debts he incurred in claiming these lands, Christian sold the Orkneys and Shetlands to Scotland in 1468.

Christian made a fresh attempt to gain the Swedish throne in 1471, only to be decisively defeated at the battle of Brunkeburg. The victor, Sten Sture, dominated Swedish politics, ruling as regent from 1501 until his death in 1503. The Swedish throne remained largely empty in the following years as the struggle to keep Sweden free from Danish rule continued with Sten Sture the Younger, who became regent in 1517. After his death in battle in 1520 Christian II of Denmark was recognized as king of Sweden.

However, instead of renewing the union, Christian II's triumph led to its final dissolution. He outraged the

ART AND ARCHITECTURE

During the 15th century the art and architecture of Sweden, Denmark, and Norway were strongly influenced by German trends due to the close trading links between the countries. Scandinavian artists of the period worked in the Gothic style, and some of their greatest achievements were elaborate carved and painted altarpieces (structures that stand behind altars). Changes in art reflecting the developments of the Italian Renaissance—in which artists copied classical (ancient Greek and Roman) art and studied the appearance of the world around them—reached Scandinavia only toward the end of the 16th century. At this time the Danish and Swedish kings invited many foreign architects, painters, sculptors, and weavers to their courts to design them magnificent new castles, furnishings, and works of art in the latest style. Among the most important of the new castles built at this time are Kronborg, Frederiksborg, and Rosenborg in Denmark and Vadstena in Sweden. Nobles also had many fine mansion houses built.

Left: Rosenborg Castle, which was designed as a summer residence for the Danish king Christian IV. The castle was built between 1603 and 1634, just outside Copenhagen. Its picturesque appearance was influenced by Flemish Renaissance architecture.

Left: A 19th-century illustration showing Gustavus Vasa rousing his Swedish countrymen to revolt against the Danes. By rallying their support and that of the free city of Lübeck, which felt threatened by Danish policy, Gustavus suceeded in expelling the Danes. He was elected king of Sweden in 1523.

Swedes by a mass execution of Sture's supporters on November 8 and 9, 1520 (called the "Stockholm Bloodbath"), and was driven out of the country by Gustavus Vasa. Gustavus, a young nobleman, ruled as King Gustavus I of Sweden from 1523 to 1560; and this time Sweden remained independent under the Vasa dynasty, which ruled the country until 1654.

THE REFORMATION

In the middle of the 16th century both Scandinavian powers responded to the Protestant Reformation that was taking place in northern Europe. In Denmark King Frederick I (ruled 1523–1533) encouraged Lutherans, and after his death in 1533 his son Christian III created a Lutheran state church. Sweden followed a similar course from 1527 to 1529 under Gustavus I. As in other countries, the new faith appealed to rulers eager to bring the church under their control and take over much of its vast wealth.

In 1592 Sweden was thrust into a union with Poland when King Sigismund of Poland, the son of King John III of Sweden, succeeded to the Swedish throne. The union between the countries brought few advantages, especially since Sigismund made an unpopular attempt to restore Catholicism in Sweden. He was deposed in 1595.

From the middle of the 16th century the balance of power between Denmark and Sweden had been slowly shifting in Sweden's favor. The Danish king Christian IV was a notable reformer and builder—he founded Christiana, later Oslo, which became the capital of Norway. However, his intervention in the Thirty Years' War (1616–1648) as the champion of European Protestantism ended in humiliation. By contrast, the victories of his young Swedish rival, Gustavus Adolphus, in the same cause made him famous throughout Europe. In the later 17th century Denmark desperately formed alliances to oppose the growing Swedish empire, while Sweden enjoyed a brilliant, brief heyday as a major European power.

SEE ALSO

♦ Germany
♦ Luther
♦ Merchants
♦ Reformation
♦ Towns
♦ Trade

Scholasticism

Scholasticism was a method of thinking that tried to combine theology (religious thought) and philosophy (which tries to explain human life and its problems). It is most closely associated with the Catholic church in medieval Europe. In the Renaissance new types of learning and thinking began to take the place of scholasticism, although it continued to shape the teachings of the Catholic church.

Scholasticism usually involved the process of debate. Typically, a master at a university would ask a question, such as whether God was the highest good. Using logic, arguments for and against were then given and discussed before the question was resolved. In this way people learned to think about issues thoroughly and to use arguments to support their position. Scholastics were particularly concerned with questions of religion. They wanted to know, for example, whether it was possible to prove that God existed. In the Christian world almost everyone believed in God. Scholastics wanted to show God existed using reasoning and logic.

Left: A 15th-century portrait of Thomas Aquinas, one of the greatest medieval scholastic thinkers. The picture is one of 28 portraits of famous men painted by the Flemish artist Justus of Ghent for Duke Federigo da Montefeltro's Renaissance court in the Italian city Urbino.

Another important issue that concerned the scholastics was what they called "universals." One group, known as Realists, believed there existed in some invisible realm the perfect examples of things (universals) that exist on earth. So although there are different types of tables or horses in the world, for example, Realists believed there also existed elsewhere

LOGIC

The most important mental tool the scholastics used was logic, which they learned chiefly from the translated writings of the ancient Greek philosopher Aristotle (384–322 B.C.). Aristotle had shown that logic has a structure like that of mathematical equations. For example, if it is the case that all birds have two wings, and that a crow is a bird, then it follows that a crow has two wings. It was this sort of method that scholastics applied to more complex questions, particularly with regard to religion.

Left: A detail from the Disputa *("Discussion"), one of a series of paintings by Raphael in the pope's library in the Vatican, Rome. The paintings show the relationship between classical learning, or logic, and the Catholic church, or faith.*

the one and only perfect table or horse. Another group of scholastics, known as Nominalists, disagreed. They thought that things existed only in the world and that universals were simply names used to describe similar things.

One of the best-known scholastics was the 12th-century French thinker Peter Abelard. He challenged the view that the Bible, because it was believed to be the word of God, could not be questioned. However, there were others who thought that the Bible and faith in general were beyond argument. They believed that because God had revealed himself through the Bible, it was not necessary to try to prove that he existed through logical reasoning.

The relationship between reason and faith was a central issue of scholasticism. The great 13th-century scholastic Thomas Aquinas wrote an enormous 21-volume work called *Summa Theologica* ("Summary of Theology"), in which he tried to show that reason and faith both have their place in the world, and that reason can be used to support the teachings of the church. However, the unity that Thomas Aquinas tried to achieve was attacked by late medieval thinkers, such as the Englishman William of Ockham, who argued that faith by its very nature is beyond the realm of reason.

DECLINE OF SCHOLASTICISM

From the 16th century fewer people were interested in the issues debated by the scholastics, who at times could descend into trivial and ridiculous arguments such as what would happen to the fish in a lake if they were excommunicated (outlawed from the church). Renaissance thinkers tended to focus on human beings and their place in the universe and less on God as revealed in the Bible. This new way of thinking became known as humanism. People were also more interested in investigating the laws of nature.

In addition, while many scholastics viewed Aristotle as the main authority for their teachings, thinkers in the Renaissance turned increasingly to Plato, his teacher. Plato's texts were translated from Greek to Latin at the start of the 16th century. Plato was more mystical and emphasized the idea of a supernatural reality, and this had a greater appeal to the Renaissance mind.

SEE ALSO

♦ Catholic Church
♦ Counter Reformation
♦ Humanism
♦ Neoplatonism

Science

During the Renaissance science was known as "natural philosophy." Most practitioners were philosophers who learned a view of the world based on the writings of the Greek philosopher Aristotle (384–322 B.C.). Much of their knowledge and understanding was theoretical and logical rather than practical. Their goal was to understand nature and to explain it, not to do experiments and make new discoveries.

According to Aristotle the universe consisted of two spheres, one inside the other. In the center was the terrestrial sphere, or the earth and sky. It was surrounded by the celestial sphere, which included the sun, planets, and stars. This celestial sphere was made up of the element ether and was perfect and unchanging.

IMPERFECT TERRESTRIAL SPHERE

In the terrestrial sphere, however, things were imperfect and changing. The terrestrial sphere was made up of four elements (earth, water, air, and fire), each of which looked for its own place in the universe. Earth, being heaviest, was at the center, surrounded by water. The lighter element of air existed above them, with the lightest element, fire, at the outer limit of the

Left: A 17th-century book illustration of the Ptolemaic system, which was based on Aristotle's incorrect but generally accepted idea that the sun, moon, and planets all orbited the earth. Copernicus challenged this system in the 16th century with his theory that the sun, not the earth, was at the center of the system.

terrestrial sphere. Everything was made up of these four basic elements modified by four qualities (hot, cold, wet, and dry).

Aristotelian physics provided a perfectly logical explanation for why the earth was at the center of the universe (because it was the heaviest element) and why the sun traveled around it (because it was in the celestial sphere, which rotated around the terrestrial sphere). The Aristotelian view of the world was written down in the second century A.D. by the Greek astronomer Ptolemy.

Aristotle's ideas formed a logical, comprehensive system that explained the whole universe. For many centuries nobody saw any reason to challenge this system, and natural philosophy consisted largely of commentaries on Aristotle. This world-view was further strengthened when Saint Thomas Aquinas adapted it to Christian beliefs in the 13th century. This meant that questioning the system might also be regarded as attacking Christianity. Changes in the 15th century, however, started the process of turning science into an activity based on observation and experiment rather than just accepting existing theories.

HUMANISM

One change was the emergence of humanism, the scholarly movement based on a love of nature and a renewed interest in the classical civilizations of the ancient Greeks and Romans. Among the Greek texts that scholars recovered were works by the philosopher Plato, the physician Galen, and the astronomer Ptolemy. The new translations of these works had a great influence on the development of science in the Renaissance. The humanist interest in nature encouraged

natural philosophers to look at the world with new eyes, rather than concentrating on theory, and a new emphasis on improving humankind fostered an optimism and confidence in human abilities.

A second change was the invention of movable type and the printing press, which meant books could be published quickly and cheaply, and ideas could spread rapidly. In the 16th century books were published about many practical trades, such as metallurgy and mining, pottery, and dyeing. They were often in everyday languages rather than in the scholarly language of Latin. People began to explore immediately useful areas such as mathematics and navigational techniques. In 1597 Gresham College was established in England to teach merchants and sailors such practical information.

Above: A 16th-century painting by Antoine Caron of astronomers observing an eclipse of the sun. Careful observation of the heavens by astronomers in the 16th century disproved many long-held beliefs about the stars and other heavenly bodies.

The fall of Constantinople in 1453 caused scholars to flee from the Turks to western Europe, bringing many Greek texts that had been preserved by Arab scholars. At first scholars tried only to produce accurate versions of the texts, which had been corrupted, but then they began taking a more practical approach. For example, the revival of Ptolemy's works on astronomy and geography encouraged overseas exploration. Columbus used Ptolemy's geography to back up his idea that it was possible to reach Asia by sailing west. The new lands, plants, animals, and peoples discovered in the Americas made philosophers reconsider the authority of classical sources, which never mentioned these things.

CHALLENGES TO ARISTOTLE

Aristotle's world-view began to be called in question as close observation of nature showed differences between theory and fact. The Polish astronomer Nicholas Copernicus (1473–1543)

EARLY EXPERIMENTS

As natural philosophers started to question the Aristotelian view of the universe, many of them began to make careful observations of what actually happened in nature and conduct experiments aimed at making new discoveries. Galileo (1564–1642) conducted many experiments connected with motion and the acceleration of falling bodies. His discoveries laid the groundwork for future work in physics by Isaac Newton (1642–1727).

One discipline that had long been devoted to experimentation was alchemy. Alchemy was based on the false idea that base metals could be turned into gold, and that the substance that could achieve this, the "elixir of life," would also cure illnesses and make people immortal. The experiments alchemists carried out in their attempts to find this elixir laid the basis for the future development of chemistry. They devised special apparatus and processes and also discovered how to make mineral acids (acids from rocks).

The Swiss alchemist and physician Paracelsus (about 1493–1541) experimented with chemicals such as mercury, sulfur, and iron to produce remedies to cure diseases—earlier medicines had been made from plants. The work of Paracelsus influenced Robert Boyle (1627–1691), who helped establish the modern science of chemistry in the 17th century.

Left: A 17th-century painting of an alchemist conducting experiments in a laboratory. Alchemy first became popular in Europe in the 12th and 13th centuries and did not finally die out until the 18th century.

challenged Aristotelian physics by placing the sun at the center of the universe, and by maintaining that the earth revolved around the sun. The Danish astronomer Tycho Brahe (1546–1601) saw a new star in 1572, and Galileo (1564–1642) observed spots on the sun and craters and mountains on the moon with the new telescope he had developed. These events threw more doubt on the Aristotelian world-view, since they showed that the celestial sphere was not unchanging, as Aristotle had claimed.

The Swiss alchemist and physician Paracelsus (about 1493–1541) rejected the theory, held by authorities such as Aristotle and Galen, that disease was caused by an imbalance in the four "humors" in the body. He urged physicians to observe the natural world and experiment for themselves. He also promoted the use of chemical medicines (see box).

In 1543 the anatomist Andreas Vesalius (1514–1564) published *De Humani Corporis Fabrica* ("On the Structure of the Human Body"), based on his own dissections. He pointed out many anatomical errors made by Galen, which had been undetected for over 1,000 years.

MANY PHILOSOPHIES

Although the Aristotelian world-view was under attack, there was no other comprehensive system to replace it. Instead, there were a variety of different ideas about natural philosophy and its purpose. Humanism and scholasticism (the system of thought that rigidly followed the teachings of the church) coexisted. There was a revival of the works of Plato and the mysterious writings of "Hermes Trismegistos," which were supposedly based on revelations made by the Egyptian god

FAMOSO·DOCTOR   PARESELSVS.

Thoth. These works promoted the idea that there were correspondences between the physical world and occult, or hidden, natural forces. This stimulated interest in "natural magic," which was considered to be a type of science requiring the understanding and manipulation of such hidden forces as gravity. Alchemy was devoted to discovering secret knowledge too, such as how to turn base metals into gold. As the 16th century ended people began to believe that they could not only discover the secrets of nature but also bend nature to their will. Natural philosophers increasingly tried to understand nature so they could control and master it for the betterment of humankind. In the early 17th century the English philosopher Francis Bacon (1561–1626) developed a methodical way of observing natural phenomena, marking the beginning of modern scientific methods.

Above: A 16th-century portrait of Paracelsus, the Swiss alchemist and physician.

SEE ALSO

♦ Alchemy
♦ Anatomy
♦ Astrology
♦ Astronomy
♦ Botany
♦ Copernicus
♦ Erasmus
♦ Galileo
♦ Magic and Superstition
♦ Mathematics
♦ Medicine and Surgery
♦ Navigation
♦ Neoplatonism
♦ Printing
♦ Technology
♦ Universities

Sculptors' Materials and Techniques

Left: A carving by the 15th-century Italian sculptor Nanni di Banco showing sculptors at work, from the guild building of Orsanmichele in Florence. The two sculptors are carving a putto (young boy) or Christ child from a block of stone.

During the Renaissance the materials and techniques used to make sculptures were very important. Unlike today, when a sculpture's value is largely determined by the fame of the artist who creates it, in the 15th and 16th centuries it was more closely related to the materials and skill with which the sculpture was made.

Renaissance sculptors worked in many kinds of material, including precious metals such as gold and silver, as well as bronze, a less valuable metal made from a mixture of copper and tin. They also used many kinds of stone, especially marble, as well as wax, clay, and different sorts of wood.

Making sculptures needed a lot of hard physical work. Master sculptors usually ran large workshops and had many assistants and apprentices to help them. They frequently worked with other craftsmen, like foundrymen—who assisted them in casting metal sculptures—and painters. Painters were involved because ever since ancient times painted or "polychrome" sculptures had been popular.

Because making sculptures was costly and time-consuming, sculptors usually needed to be asked, or commissioned, to make something before they started work. The sculptor provided the customer—known as the patron—with a drawing or sometimes a small-scale model of what the sculpture would look like. If the model met with the patron's approval, the sculptor and patron signed a legal contract. In the contract the patron was often very specific about the kind and quality of the material the sculpture was to be made from.

GOLD, SILVER, AND BRONZE

The most precious materials used to make sculptures were gold and silver. They were often crafted into statuettes (small statues) of holy figures for wealthy people or into elaborate decorations for their homes, like the saltcellar made by the 16th-century artist Benvenuto Cellini (see Volume 3, page 21). Larger sculptures made from materials like wood or bronze were sometimes gilded (coated with gold) to make them look like solid gold without the expense.

Bronze was one of the most widely used materials for sculpture during the Renaissance. Sculptors made small objects like medals and statuettes from it, as well as life-size statues and large sculpted panels for altars and cathedral doors. Bronze had been used for sculptures since ancient times, and in the 15th century Italian sculptors like Ghiberti and Donatello tried to create

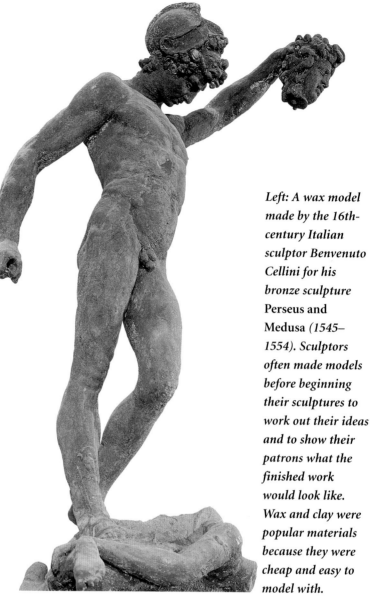

Left: A wax model made by the 16th-century Italian sculptor Benvenuto Cellini for his bronze sculpture **Perseus and Medusa** *(1545–1554). Sculptors often made models before beginning their sculptures to work out their ideas and to show their patrons what the finished work would look like. Wax and clay were popular materials because they were cheap and easy to model with.*

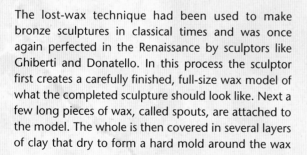

THE LOST-WAX TECHNIQUE

The lost-wax technique had been used to make bronze sculptures in classical times and was once again perfected in the Renaissance by sculptors like Ghiberti and Donatello. In this process the sculptor first creates a carefully finished, full-size wax model of what the completed sculpture should look like. Next a few long pieces of wax, called spouts, are attached to the model. The whole is then covered in several layers of clay that dry to form a hard mold around the wax

model. Molten bronze is then poured into the spouts. The hot metal melts the wax and fills the space left behind as the wax seeps away. Once the metal cools, the clay casing is broken to reveal the statue inside. The sculptor then files and polishes the surface of the metal to make it smooth. To reduce the amount of bronze used, a wooden or clay core can be made for the wax model so that the finished sculpture is hollow. Large sculptures are often made in several parts.

works as refined as those that survived from ancient Rome. They perfected methods of metal casting, particularly the lost-wax technique (see box on page 39).

STONE AND MARBLE

Sculptors worked in many kinds of stone, but by far the most prized was marble. Marble is a kind of crystallized limestone and is very hard and dense. Ancient Greek and Roman sculptors often used marble because it could be polished smooth and was hard-wearing. In the Renaissance the best and most expensive marble came from quarries in the Carrara region of Italy, close to Pisa.

Carving sculptures from a block of marble required a large number of tools. Sculptors first used hammers and chisels to create the rough shape of the statue. They then used increasingly smaller tools to carve the finer details. Most sculptors then polished the marble to create a smooth surface. A few artists, like Donatello, sometimes preferred to leave the surface rough.

Before they went to work on the marble, sculptors often began by making a small-scale model of the statue in wax or clay. They then used the model as a reference as they carved out the full-size statue. In the early 16th century Michelangelo began the practice of making a full-size model in clay and then leaving much of the carving—and hard work—to his assistants. Only when the sculpture was nearly complete did he make the final, finishing touches.

WOOD AND TERRACOTTA

During the Renaissance sculptors continued to make wooden statues, just as they had in medieval times. In northern Europe, where there were

Left: An unfinished sculpture known as the Atlas Slave *(about 1516) by Michelangelo and assistants. The sculpture was intended to be part of an ambitious project for Pope Julius II's tomb. It shows how sculptors carved away unwanted stone and used increasingly fine tools as they crafted the shape of the sculpture.*

many forests and plentiful supplies of timber, wood was the most popular material. German sculptors often carved wooden statues of Christ and the saints as well as intricate altarpieces depicting scenes from the Bible. In Italy there was less timber available, and woods that were good for carving were expensive. Nevertheless, sculptors often preferred to work with wood because it was much easier to carve than stone.

During the 1440s the Florentine sculptor Luca della Robbia (about 1399–1442) used a new material to make sculptures called terracotta (Italian for "baked clay"). Terracotta was widely used to make pottery, but della Robbia was one of the first artists to use it for sculpture. He modeled clay into sculptures, which he then fired in a kiln. He painted the fired sculptures in colorful glazes (made from tin and lead oxides) and refired them. Glazed terracotta sculptures soon became popular throughout Europe.

Sculpture

During the Renaissance there were many different kinds of sculpture. Sculptors made life-size statues to stand in public squares as well as small statuettes for wealthy collectors. They carved monuments, tombs, and pulpits in churches and cathedrals, and medals and busts (portraits showing the head and shoulders) for powerful men and women. Some of these types of sculpture were new or had not been made since ancient times.

Although sculptors in the 14th century based their work on medieval traditions, by the 15th century Italian artists began to experiment with new types of sculpture, materials, and subjects. Above all, Renaissance sculptors, like Renaissance painters, aimed to renew the spirit of classical (ancient Greek and Roman) art by creating works that were lifelike and centered on the portrayal of the human body.

A NEW TRADITION

According to the Italian sculptor Lorenzo Ghiberti (1378–1455), Renaissance sculpture first began to develop in Italy at the beginning of the 15th century. It was at this time, Ghiberti argued, that he and other sculptors working in Florence began to revive and imitate classical art and to work in a more lifelike style. Ghiberti viewed the art of the

Below: Judith and Holofernes *(about 1446–1460), a bronze sculpture by the great 15th-century sculptor Donatello.*

preceding age—the Middle Ages—as inferior to that of his own time. Renaissance scholars described art from the Middle Ages as "Gothic" after the Germanic peoples called Goths who had overrun the western Roman Empire in the fourth century A.D.

Today art historians still use the term Gothic to describe art made in Europe mainly between the 12th and 14th centuries. Some Gothic artists did, in fact, look back to classical sculpture for inspiration. In the main, however, Gothic art was inward-looking and spiritual, and was not concerned with the lifelike depiction of people and the world around them. Gothic was one of the most successful and long-lived styles in the history of art. Both painters and sculptors continued to work in Gothic styles throughout the 15th century and beyond, especially in countries outside Italy.

GHIBERTI'S BAPTISTERY DOORS

Most scholars agree with Ghiberti that Italian sculpture underwent a dramatic transformation in the early 15th century. The initial spark for this change came in 1401 in the city of Florence, when the Guild of Cloth Importers organized a competition to find an artist to make a pair of doors for the baptistery, a building that was part of the city's cathedral complex. The doors were to be decorated with

Right: Scenes from the Story of Joseph (1425–1452), one of 10 panels from the second set of doors made by Ghiberti for the baptistery in Florence. The elegant poses and dress of the figures are influenced by classical art, as is the design of the buildings. Ghiberti created a lifelike sense of depth in the panel by using perspective, a recently discovered mathematical system that helped artists show three-dimensional space.

bronze relief sculptures (sculpted panels) that showed stories taken from the Old Testament. The guild invited sculptors to submit a bronze relief showing the Sacrifice of Isaac.

Seven artists submitted panels, including Filippo Brunelleschi and Ghiberti, who was young and relatively unknown at the time. Ghiberti won the competition and spent the following 50 years working on this first pair of doors for the baptistery as well as a second pair. He gained an increasingly deeper understanding of Roman art and aimed to revive its qualities.

CLASSICAL INSPIRATION

Throughout the 15th century sculptors studied and were inspired by ancient Greek and Roman sculpture. Much

classical sculpture survived into the Renaissance, and new building work in Rome and other cities also unearthed more ancient treasures. Renaissance scholars, artists, and collectors—including Ghiberti, the painter Andrea Mantegna, the Medici family in Florence, and the popes in Rome—were able to create fine collections of classical statues, busts, reliefs, medals, and statuettes. Some of these types of sculpture had not been made since Roman times, and Italian sculptors set out to revive them.

DONATELLO'S PIONEERING WORK

The Florentine sculptor Donatello (1386–1466) pioneered many new types of sculpture. He was a pupil of Ghiberti and worked with him on the baptistery doors. Today most scholars agree that Donatello was the greatest sculptor of the 15th century. He was never content simply to imitate classical art but wanted his own sculpture to be even better than ancient examples. Donatello introduced a new kind of relief, called *relievo stacciato* (Italian for "flattened relief"), which was unknown in the ancient world. In this sort of carving the sculptor cut away only a tiny amount of the stone's surface to create a delicate sculpture more like a drawing than a traditional, deeply cut relief sculpture.

Donatello was also the first Western artist since Roman times to make free-standing life-size sculptures. One of the finest of them was displayed in the garden of the Medici Palace and depicted the biblical heroine Judith about to strike off the head of Holofernes (see page 41). His sculpture of the Old Testament hero David was even more famous (see Volume 5, page 24). Making such sculptures—especially out of bronze—demanded a great deal of technical as well as artistic skill.

COMPETITION AND INSPIRATION

Later sculptors competed with Donatello to create impressive, lifelike statues. They included Andrea del Verrocchio (about 1435–1488), who ran one of the largest artist's workshops in Florence. His best-known works include bronze sculptures of David, a fountain with a putto (young boy) holding a dolphin, and the *Colleoni Monument* (see box on page 44).

Donatello and other Renaissance sculptors were inspired by small Roman statues known as statuettes. These statuettes usually showed the gods and heroes described in classical myths and were highly prized by Renaissance collectors. Soon Italian sculptors like Il Riccio, Giambologna, and Benvenuto Cellini were making their own bronze statuettes.

One of the functions of Renaissance art was to celebrate famous or powerful people. Sculptors made a variety of sculptures to commemorate, or record, individuals. They included busts that portrayed peoples' features in a lifelike way, medals that commemorated events such as a marriage or victory in war, and tombs and monuments.

MADONNAS

Despite the new variety of artworks in Renaissance Italy, the vast majority of sculptures continued to show religious subjects. Especially popular were small relief carvings of the Virgin Mary and Christ child, known as the Madonna and Child (Madonna is Italian for "My Lady"). Mary had become an increasingly important figure for Christians since the Middle Ages, and they often prayed to her as a go-between between themselves and God. Sculptures of the Madonna and Child were displayed in churches, in homes, and on the walls of alleyways and streets. One of the most brilliant makers of sculpted Madonnas was the Florentine artist Luca della Robbia (about 1399–1482). During the 1440s he began to make reliefs out of terracotta (baked clay) coated with hard-wearing glazes (made from tin or lead oxide), materials that had previously been used for pottery. Della Robbia painted his sculptures bright colors, especially sky blue and creamy white.

Above: **The Madonna and Child with Two Angels,** *a glazed terracotta relief made by Luca della Robbia in about 1450.*

EQUESTRIAN MONUMENTS

An equestrian monument is a type of statue that portrays a person on horseback. One of the most spectacular ancient monuments to survive in Renaissance Rome was the life-size bronze equestrian monument of the emperor Marcus Aurelius (see Volume 1, page 27). For centuries people had regarded the statue with awe because of its size, lifelikeness, and costliness, as well as the technical expertise needed to make it.

In 15th-century Italy, as sculptors gradually became more skillful at casting large-scale bronze statues, they began to create equestrian monuments to rival the ancient statues. Donatello and Verrocchio both produced remarkable equestrian monuments. Donatello's statue *Gatta-melata* (see Volume 3, page 30) in Padua is majestic and menacing, while Verrocchio's *Colleoni Monument* in Venice is full of fierce energy. Verrocchio was determined to outstrip even Donatello and showed his horse with one foot in the air, a real demonstration of skill since the horse's slender legs are all that support the heavy statue. Leonardo da Vinci also dreamed of creating an equestrian monument. He was more ambitious than even Verrocchio and wanted to show a rider on a rearing horse. However, Leonardo was unable to solve the technical problems involved, and the monument was never made.

Below: Verrocchio's **Colleoni Monument** *(1481–1496), made to commemorate the Italian soldier Bartolommeo Colleoni.*

The first sculptor to make a portrait bust since Roman times was the Florentine artist Mino da Fiesole (1429–1489), who in 1453 portrayed the Florentine ruler Piero de Medici. Another Florentine sculptor, Antonio Rossellino (1427–1479), carved some very lifelike busts that also suggest the personalities of the people they show.

In the 15th century the Italian artist Antonio Pisanello revived another type of sculpted portrait that had been popular in ancient times: the medal. Medals often included a profile portrait (a side view of the face) of a ruler or some other famous individual. On the reverse there was usually a picture symbolizing the individual's achievements or marking a special event in their life. The duke of Ferrara, Leonello d'Este (1407–1450), had many medals made and was largely responsible for making them a popular art form.

Renaissance sculptors also began to make a new type of tomb that was set against a wall rather than lying on the floor, which is how medieval tombs were designed. Usually a sculpted effigy (image) of the dead person was shown as if asleep on a stone bier (a bedlike platform) set between two columns. Above was a carving that often showed the Virgin and Child, while below was the tomb itself. The first such tombs were made for humanist scholars, but popes and other rulers were also commemorated in this way.

MANNERISM AND BEYOND
By the end of the 15th century Italian sculptors were highly skilled at making lifelike sculptures inspired by classical examples. The sculptors of the 16th century then began to take sculpture in new directions, working in a style scholars now call "mannerism." Their sculptures often show the human form in complicated poses, sometimes with exaggerated proportions to create a sense of energy, power, or grace.

The first sculptor to begin working in this way was Michelangelo (1475–1564). His most famous work is the painted ceiling of the Sistine Chapel, but he always considered himself a sculptor first and foremost. He became

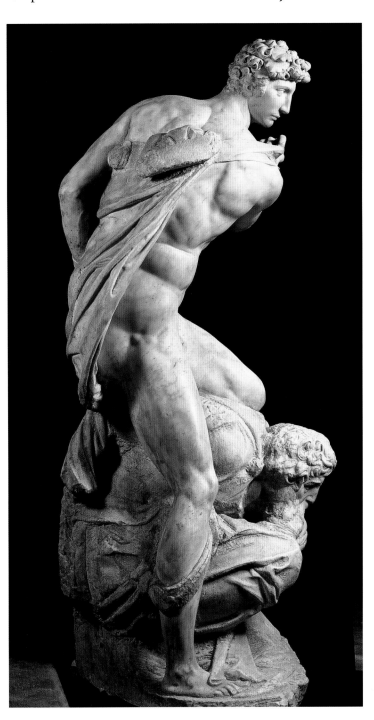

Below: **Victory,** *a sculpture made by Michelangelo in 1527–1530 for the tomb of Pope Julius II. The twisting arrangement of the figures influenced many later artists.*

WOODEN SCULPTURE IN NORTHERN EUROPE

In northern European countries, where there were many forests and timber was plentiful, sculptors specialized in carving wood. There were particularly strong traditions of wood carving in southern Germany, especially in the cities of Nuremberg and Würzburg, from where two of the best-known sculptors came: Tilman Riemenschneider (about 1460–1531) and Veit Stoss (about 1450–1530). German sculptors remained largely untouched by Italian art and continued working in a Gothic style until well into the 16th century. They often used wood from the common lime, or linden, because it was easier to carve than other hardwoods like oak and walnut, and until around 1500 they usually painted their sculptures. Some of their finest carvings are intricate altarpieces.

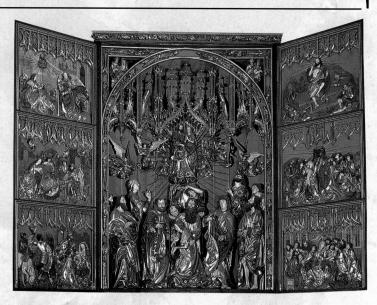

Above: A painted wooden altarpiece (1477–1489) by Veit Stoss in the church of Saint Mary in Kraków, Poland. It shows scenes from the life of the Virgin and her Assumption (when she enters heaven).

well known in 1503 when he completed a huge marble statue of David—at 18 ft (5.5m) tall, it was the largest figure sculpture carved since ancient times. Michelangelo's ability to carve the human form and to express ideas and emotions like strength, power, beauty, and suffering through his sculptures was greatly admired both by other artists and by patrons (the people who ordered and paid for works of art).

Inspired by Michelangelo, other sculptors working in the 16th century often devised complex poses for their statues in order to display their skill. *Contrapposto* is a term used to describe a pose in which one part of the body twists away from another. Earlier Renaissance artists, like the classical sculptors of Greece and Rome, had used a gentle form of *contrapposto* to give their statues a relaxed, natural appearance. Mannerist sculptors liked to show the body in complex, twisting poses that expressed violent energy and movement as well as showing off their artistic skill. These tendencies can best be seen in the work of two well-known Mannerist sculptors: Giambologna and Benvenuto Cellini.

ITALIAN IDEAS SPREAD ABROAD

During the 16th century Italian Renaissance sculpture became known across Europe. Some Italian sculptors went to work in foreign courts, where their work inspired other artists. In 1540, for example, Cellini became court artist to the king of France, Francis I. Under his influence French sculptors such as Jean Goujon (about 1510–1568) created masterpieces that blended Italian mannerism with their native styles.

Sforza Family

The Sforza were a prominent Italian family of condottieri (hired soldiers) who took control of the city-state of Milan in 1450 and ruled it for almost a hundred years. Two of the most famous members of the family were Francesco Sforza (1401–1466), the military commander who first seized power in Milan, and Ludovico Sforza (1452–1508), who as duke of Milan was a great patron of the arts and established one of the most brilliant courts in Renaissance Italy.

The first Sforza, Muzio Attendolo (1369–1424), was one of Italy's leading condottieri. He is said to have acquired the family name by his use of the word *sforzato*, meaning "by force." The Sforza came from the Romagna, in the Papal States; but as mercenary soldiers they served many masters—the pope, Milan, Florence, and Naples. When Muzio drowned during a battle in 1424, his son Francesco took over command of his troops and showed his own military ability by defeating his father's enemies.

In 1431 Francesco Sforza was created commander of Milan's army by the duke of Milan, Filippo Maria

Above: Francesco Sforza, depicted on a 15th-century bronze medallion. As a mercenary soldier, Francesco was given command of Milan's army in 1431. But his uneasy relationship with Milan's duke made him change sides several times before he eventually seized control of the city and made himself duke of Milan in 1450.

Visconti. Francesco was an excellent commander, but the duke did not want to give too much authority to such a ruthless and ambitious man. To bind the commander to him more closely, the duke agreed to engage Bianca Maria, his only daughter, to Francesco, but then tried to delay the marriage. In the end Francesco managed to persuade him to change his mind by winning several victories for his enemies.

Relations between the two men remained uneasy until 1447, when the dying Filippo once again appealed to Francesco for help against the advancing Venetian army. Francesco responded, but the duke died before he arrived. Instead of installing a new duke, the Milanese people declared their city a republic. At first Francesco accepted the situation and won several victories against the Venetians. But when he was not given overall command, and he realized that the Milanese did not trust him, he declared war on the republic, besieged Milan, and in February 1450 entered the city in triumph as its new duke.

Francesco wanted to make his position secure rather than fight more battles. In April 1454 he made peace with Venice at Lodi, and the following

MILAN AND THE VISCONTI

By the 15th century Milan dominated the fertile north Italian plain. The region, known as Lombardy, was very important because it controlled the Alpine passes leading into Italy. Milan itself was large and prosperous thanks to its textile manufactures—wool, cotton, and silk—and a metalworking industry based on armor and weapons.

From about 1300 Milan was ruled by the Visconti family, who became hereditary dukes and pursued a policy of expansion that often brought them into conflict with the powerful republics of Florence and Venice. The Visconti were a family of Milanese nobles—their name means "viscounts." By the early 14th century they were preeminent in Milan, but their possessions were scattered. Then, in 1385 Gian Galeazzo Visconti put his uncle Bernabo in prison, where he later died, leaving Gian Galeazzo free to concentrate power in his own hands. He embarked on a determined and successful expansion all the way across the north of Italy to the Adriatic. Gian Galeazzo made himself duke of Milan and seemed destined to create a great north Italian kingdom. In 1402 he invaded Tuscany, and he was about to strike at an encircled Florence when he died suddenly. Many of his conquests were lost during the disastrous rule of his eldest son Giovanni Maria, but Milan remained strong during the long reign of his younger son Filippo Maria Visconti (ruled 1412–1447).

year he became one of the architects of the Italian League, a triple alliance of Milan, Venice, and Florence aimed at stabilizing the situation in Italy. Joined a year later by the papacy and Naples, this alliance kept the peace and ensured that there would be no foreign intervention in the peninsula.

Francesco died in 1466 and was succeeded by his 22-year-old son Galeazzo Maria Sforza. He is generally considered a less skilful diplomat than his father, though it is possible that rivalries between Italian states were too strong to be bound by the agreement made at Lodi. Milan became aligned with Florence, while Venice and Naples reached an agreement. However, a reasonable balance of power was maintained for Galeazzo's reign.

LUDOVICO'S COURT

In 1476 the duke was assassinated, and his seven-year-old son Gian Galeazzo succeeded him. The boy's mother, the Duchess Bona, ruled as regent until 1479, when she was thrust aside by his uncle, Ludovico Sforza. Called *Il Moro* ("the Moor") because of his dark complexion, Ludovico was politically able and a great patron of the arts. Many leading figures, including Leonardo da Vinci and the architect Donato Bramante, were attracted to his court, which was one of the most splendid in Renaissance Italy.

Left: A 15th-century portrait of Galeazzo Maria Sforza (1444–1476), duke of Milan. Galeazzo Maria was a despotic ruler who nevertheless brought benefits to Milan by encouraging trade, introducing rice cultivation, and building canals.

Ludovico kept his grip on power even when Gian Galeazzo was old enough to rule. The duke's wife resented the situation, and Ludovico feared that she would persuade her father, King Alfonso of Naples, to move against him. In order to prevent this, Ludovico encouraged the French king Charles VIII to assert his claim to Naples. Once Charles was sure that the Milanese would not oppose his passage over the Alps, he led an invading army into Italy. While he made a triumphant march down the peninsula, Gian Galeazzo fell sick and died. Many people suspected that Ludovico, who promptly took the title duke of Milan, had had his nephew poisoned.

After Charles VIII's easy conquest of Naples Ludovico joined an alliance led by Venice to drive the French king out of Italy. However, following the example of the French, there were interventions by other European powers, which eventually took over the peninsula. Ludovico himself suffered the consequences.

LUDOVICO'S FALL

Charles VIII's successor to the French throne, Louis XII, had a claim to Milan and decided to enforce it. Ludovico found himself isolated as Louis gained the support of Venice and the heavily taxed Milanese people. In 1499 Milan fell into the hands of the French, and Ludovico fled to Germany. In 1500 he briefly recovered Milan, only to be captured and to spend the last eight years of his life as a French prisoner.

From this time onward Milan was a territory disputed between France and the Hapsburg emperor Charles V. Ludovico's son Massimiliano managed to hold power briefly (1512–1515), as did another son, Francesco, from 1521 to 1524. In 1529 Francesco was reinstalled as ruler of Milan by Charles V, who had driven the French out of Italy, but only as a Hapsburg puppet. The Sforza ruling line ended with Francesco's death in 1535, and Milan became, and remained for several centuries, a Hapsburg possession.

Above: This 16th-century book illustration shows Massimiliano Sforza dining in his garden with his family.

LEONARDO IN MILAN

In 1482 Leonardo da Vinci was sent to Milan as a friendly gesture by the ruler of Florence, Lorenzo de Medici. On his arrival Leonardo presented Ludovico Sforza with a silver lute he had designed. Leonardo decided to settle at the Milanese court and over the following 17 years he served Ludovico in many capacities, designing court festivals as well as painting and working as a civil and military engineer. During this period he began keeping his famous notebooks and painted several of his best-known pictures, including *The Last Supper* and two versions of *The Virgin of the Rocks*. Leonardo's contemporaries were most enthusiastic about his life-size clay model of a horse, which was destroyed after the French captured Milan in 1499. Leonardo left after the fall of Ludovico, but later returned to spend another five years in the city.

Shakespeare

Above: A copy of a 16th-century portrait of Shakespeare, aged 34. Shakespeare was the third of eight children born to a glove-maker and a farmer's daughter. Despite these humble beginnings, he grew up to become a renowned poet and playwright.

William Shakespeare (1564–1616) was an English playwright, poet, and actor who lived in Elizabeth I's reign, when drama was undergoing a radical transformation. From being performed on carts by traveling players, drama was moving into permanent playhouses, where it was performed by resident companies of actors. Shakespeare joined one of these companies in London and started writing plays for the company to perform. He earned himself a reputation—rarely disputed to this day—as the greatest playwright in the English language.

When Shakespeare was born in the small English market town of Stratford-upon Avon, Elizabeth I had been on the throne for six years. She had already begun to inspire a cultural rebirth throughout her realm. While he was still at school, William would have seen the pageants and shows that were put on in Stratford by traveling companies of professional actors.

A CAREER IN THE THEATER

At the age of 18 Shakespeare married Anne Hathaway, who was eight years older than he was. During the next two years they had three children, and it was probably shortly after this that Shakespeare moved to London, where he took up acting. By 1592 he was a successful actor and had already written several plays.

From 1592 to 1594 London's theaters were closed because of the plague, and during this time Shakespeare wrote two long poems, *Venus and Adonis* and *Lucrece*. When the theaters reopened, he became a "sharer" in a new company called the Chamberlain's Men, which meant that he received a share of the company's earnings. By 1598 the Chamberlain's Men were doing so well that they were able to build their own theater in Southwark on the south bank of the Thames River, naming it the Globe.

THE GLOBE THEATER

The Globe Theater was a round, wooden building open to the sky. The audience stood in the pit in front of the stage (where they got wet if it rained) or sat in roofed galleries around it. The

SHAKESPEARE'S PLAYS

Shakespeare was not only an outstandingly gifted playwright, he was also an extremely prolific one. In the space of about 20 years he wrote almost two plays a year. His plays included histories, comedies, tragedies, and tragicomedies, all written in blank verse. Blank verse is a type of verse without rhymes, and Shakespeare used a line with five stressed syllables in it. An example is the first line of Hamlet's famous speech, "To be, or not to be. That is the question."

Shakespeare's history plays were a way of informing his audience about relatively recent English history. His three parts of *Henry VI* and the play *Richard III* cover the history of the Wars of the Roses. Henry VII, who was Elizabeth I's grandfather, had seized the crown from Richard III in battle and in fact had rather a shaky claim to the throne. By making Richard a wicked tyrant in his play, Shakespeare made it seem that Henry was justified in killing him and taking the throne.

Shakespeare's comedies, such as *Love's Labours Lost*, *As You Like It*, *The Taming of the Shrew*, and *A Midsummer Night's Dream*, are essentially lighthearted love stories. In some of his comedies Shakespeare introduced an added interest by having the heroine dress up as a man for some of the action. Since there were no women actors in Shakespeare's day, the part of the heroine would be played by a boy. So the audience would be watching a boy pretending to be a woman pretending to be a man.

Shakespeare's greatest plays are his tragedies— *Hamlet*, *Othello*, *King Lear*, and *Macbeth*. In all of them a great man is brought low by a fatal flaw of character. The Scottish play *Macbeth* was written to honor James I, the king of Scotland who became king of England in 1603. James was particularly interested in witchcraft, and Shakespeare wrote three witches into the play to please the new king.

Right: A scene from the history play Henry V, *performed in a reconstructed Globe Theater on the south bank of the Thames River in London. In Shakespeare's day all the women's parts would have been performed by boy actors.*

stage was built on different levels, so different kinds of scenes could be shown. Over the stage was a roof and a so-called hut, which contained machinery for special effects. Gods could be lowered through a trapdoor, shooting stars could appear, and thunder and lightning were common effects.

Shakespeare wrote many sonnets during his lifetime, and in 1609 a book of his sonnets was published. Around 1610 he retired from the stage. He then spent more time back in Stratford, where he had bought a large house. He died there in 1616 and was buried in Stratford parish church.

Ships

Left: A 19th-century painting showing Ferdinand Magellan's fleet of caravels navigating the Magellan Strait at the tip of South America in 1520. The caravel usually had three or four masts, carrying square sails on the two forward masts and a lateen, or triangular, sail on the third and fourth.

The Renaissance period saw revolutionary changes in the design of European ships. In the Middle Ages trade routes in the Mediterranean were plied by low-sided galleys that were frequently rowed for much of the journey. For longer routes in northern Europe a small merchant vessel called the cog was used. These ships had only one or two masts to carry sails, which meant they could not sail very fast. By 1500 ships were full-rigged, with three masts and as many as eight sails. These much more seaworthy vessels were faster and more suitable for sailing long distances. They enabled the great explorers to make their revolutionary voyages of discovery.

One of the first of the new vessels was the caravel, which was about 80 ft (24m) long. Originally it had two

masts, but this was soon increased to three. The two forward masts had square sails, and there was a lateen (triangular) sail on the third. The lateen sail, based on the one used on the Arab dhow, made it possible to sail closer to the wind, making the ship faster and more maneuverable.

Caravels were used by Christopher Columbus for his voyage to the Americas and by Batholomeu Dias when he rounded the Cape of Good Hope. Ferdinand Magellan also set out with a fleet of caravels on his epic voyage around the world.

The carrack was larger than the caravel and more robust. It was a three-masted vessel that probably originated in the Italian port of Genoa. Carracks were essentially trading ships that plied between the Mediterranean and northern Europe. They had a high forecastle (a structure built on the fore

LIFE ON BOARD

Life on board the sailing ships of the 16th century was hard and uncomfortable. Only the captain and officers could expect any privacy, in tiny cabins built on deck. The rest of the crew bedded down on the deck at night. The hours of the day and night were marked out by sand clocks, which measured every half-hour. The passage of time was called out by ships' boys. When they were not on duty or sleeping, the sailors might be gambling (prohibited, but tolerated) or attending morning or evening prayers.

The high point of the day was the one meal, even though food on board ship was scarce and unappetizing. If they were lucky, Spanish sailors could expect fish, oil, rice, and wine, while their English counterparts made do with beef, butter, and beer. All sailors, however, relied on "hardtack"—baked ship's biscuit, which was stale, hard, and usually infested with weevils. Fresh fruit and vegetables were nonexistent unless the ship had just entered or left port, and diseases such as scurvy and dysentery were common.

Below: Present-day junks sailing on the Li River in China. The junk is a flat-bottomed boat that carries four-sided sails made out of matting stiffened with bamboo. In the 15th century the junk was one of the most seaworthy vessels in the world.

deck), which was used for accommodation and storage. But as the forecastle became more elaborate, it began to catch the wind, making the ship less maneuverable.

A LONGER AND LEANER SHIP
The carrack's successor, the galleon, was built without the high forecastle. It was a longer and leaner ship than the carrack, making it both more stable and more maneuverable. These large vessels had three, or even four, masts, each carrying several sails. Fully rigged,

these ships were no longer so dependent on fair winds; they could tack into the wind, as well as sail with it. The galleon was originally developed as a warship—in 1588 Philip II of Spain sent an armada of ships that included many galleons to try to invade England. But by the end of the 16th century galleons were becoming the main type of trading ship.

In China travel and trade depended on the junk. The design of the junk was a flat-bottomed wooden box, with a centerline-mounted rudder that gave

precise control. The junk was built to be very strong; solid planked walls, called bulkheads, ran both longways and crosswise through the ship, strengthening the structure and protecting it against damage. It had up to five masts that carried sails made of matting stiffened with bamboo battens. Despite their ungainly appearance, in the early 15th century junks had developed into the largest, strongest, and most seaworthy ships in the world.

WARSHIPS WITH MOUNTED GUNS

In the Middle Ages little distinction was made between merchant ships and warships. In times of war temporary wooden castles (structures) were added to the bow and stern of ordinary ships, providing platforms for archers and slingers. By the middle of the 14th century English, French, and Spanish ships were using mounted guns—relatively small weapons located in the fore and aft castles. At first the guns were mounted on a rigid timber bed and could only fire forward over the bow of the ship. By the late 15th century sliding mounts had been introduced that enabled the gun to be maneuvered into other positions. By the 16th century some larger ships were carrying cast-iron cannons that could

fire a 60-pound (27-kg) solid shot. These cannon-armed warships could cover vast distances—as early as the 1520s the Spanish were patrolling Caribbean waters in a fleet of ships armed with cannon.

Henry VII of England created the first oceangoing battle fleet. His son, Henry VIII, introduced gunports in battle ships. They were portholes located along the side of the ship that enabled heavy guns to be mounted low in the ship, making the vessel more stable. A typical 16th-century warship carried a great range of weaponry, including short-barreled, short-range cannons and a number of guns that fired lighter shot over a longer range. Henry VIII's best-known warship, the *Henry Grâce à Dieu*, had 186 guns.

These great men-of-war did not completely supplant the old warships powered by oars. At the battle of Lepanto in 1571, fought between the Turks and a combined European fleet, cannon-armed galleys were propelled by between 50 to 200 oarsmen. The Europeans also fielded six Venetian galleasses, huge ships that depended on sails as well as oars. Although they were difficult to maneuver, their concentrated firepower was crucial to the European victory.

Above: The battle of Lepanto, depicted in a 16th-century painting. At this decisive battle fought in the Mediterranean in 1571 the Turkish fleet was defeated by a combined force of oar-powered galleys armed with cannon together with six galleasses, which had sails as well as oars and carried a battery of heavy guns.

SEE ALSO

♦ Exploration
♦ Maps and
   Mapmaking
♦ Navigation
♦ Portugal
♦ Trade
♦ Transportation
♦ Warfare

Sigismund

Sigismund of Luxembourg (1368–1437) was one of the most influential rulers in Renaissance Europe. Largely through marriage and family connections he became the king not only of Hungary in 1387 but also of Germany in 1410 and Bohemia (in present-day Czech Republic) in 1419. In 1433 he became Holy Roman emperor. For most of his life he was engaged in struggles to expand his power or defend his lands against his enemies. His greatest achievement was his part in ending the Great Schism (1378–1417), the split in the Catholic church during which rival popes claimed to be its supreme head.

Sigismund was born near Nuremberg in Germany in 1368. His father was the Holy Roman emperor Charles IV, who died when his son was only 10 years old. Sigismund grew up into an intelligent young man who could speak four languages. He was tall and good-looking, wearing his hair fashionably long. At the age of 17 he married Maria, the daughter of the king of Hungary. On the death of her father Maria became queen, and in 1387 Sigismund was crowned king consort.

One of the first major tests of Sigismund's rule came in 1395, when the Ottoman Turks invaded Hungary. He quickly organized a coalition of French, German, and other European forces to fight the Muslim enemy. In the following year the two sides met in battle at Nicopolis on the banks of the Danube River in present-day Bulgaria. Although Sigismund was personally

Left: This portrait of Sigismund was painted in 1433 by the Italian artist Pisanello (1395–1455). Sigismund was the last Holy Roman emperor from the royal house of Luxembourg.

brave, he could be indecisive as a leader, and the allies lacked coordination on the field of battle. As a result the Turkish sultan Bayezid I routed the Christians, killing and capturing thousands. Sigismund himself barely escaped with his life. Fortunately for the Christian cause, the Ottomans then had to deal with an invasion of Mongol armies from central Asia.

THE COUNCIL OF CONSTANCE

Fourteen years after the catastrophe Sigismund became king of Germany in 1410, and in the following years he turned his attention to the Great Schism. He persuaded one of the rival popes to hold a council at the city of Constance in Germany to sort out the split in the Catholic church that had

brought it into such bad repute. In 1417, after three years of negotiations, the schism came to an end when the rivals were replaced by a single candidate who was elected Pope Martin V (pope 1417–1431). During the council Sigismund earned the hatred of the people of Bohemia for allowing the Czech religious reformer Jan Hus (about 1372–1415) to be condemned at the council and burned at the stake— even though Sigismund had promised Hus that he would protect him.

WAR AGAINST THE HUSSITES

Sigismund spent most of the rest of his life fighting against the Hussites (the Bohemian supporters of Hus) as well as fending off the Turks in Hungary. To help his cause against the Hussites, he persuaded Pope Martin to proclaim a crusade against them in 1420. But under their leader Jan Zizka the Hussites fought with great courage and repeatedly defeated Sigismund. Indeed, they were so successful that they advanced out of their homeland of Bohemia into German territories. In 1431 a further crusade was launched against them, but it also failed. Sigismund decided to urge the pope to call a council at Basel in Switzerland to come to terms with the Hussites. In 1436 an agreement was drawn up under which the Bohemians were allowed some freedom of worship in return for recognizing Sigismund as their king (he had actually inherited the crown in 1419). Sigismund was only able to enjoy the new-found loyalty of his Bohemian citizens for a year before he died in 1437.

Above: This 15th-century illustration shows Sigismund in conference with his allies against the Turks in 1396.

SEE ALSO

♦ Bohemia
♦ Catholic Church
♦ Eastern Europe
♦ Holy Roman Empire
♦ Martin V
♦ Papacy
♦ Religious Dissent

Social Order

By the beginning of the Renaissance period the strict divisions of medieval society were starting to break down. While most people still stayed in the social group in which they had been born, commercial and economic expansion brought new opportunities for talented and ambitious people to rise up the social hierarchy.

In the Middle Ages society was divided into three "estates." The third estate, which made up the majority of the population, consisted of the commoners—peasants and craftsmen. The second estate consisted of the nobles, who had numerous privileges but also obligations, such as the duty of protecting the commoners on their land. The first estate was made up of the educated clergy. The only way for a commoner to improve his place in the social order was by joining the church. The church would provide him with an education and the opportunity to rise through the ranks of the clergy.

By the 14th century wealthy commoners were beginning to appear as prosperity increased, and with wealth came social status. The church lost its monopoly on learning; the growth of schools and universities across Europe made education accessible to people outside the church. The nobility began to intermarry with wealthy commoners. It became possible for people to advance their careers at royal courts without necessarily being of noble birth. The medieval notion of the three estates had become out of date.

Left: A 15th-century book illustration showing peasants working in the fields of their lord, as they were obliged to do for a certain number of days every month. The lord's castle can be seen in the background.

As society became more mobile, attempts were made to keep people in their place. One method was through laws, called sumptuary laws, that regulated the way that people dressed. These laws tried to make sure that people did not wear clothing inappropriate to their station in life. The Augsburg ordinance of 1537, for example, decreed that everyone should wear clothing suitable to their status.

THE NEWLY RICH

Merchants and bankers were the most socially mobile group in the Renaissance. They often started from humble beginnings—as peddlers or craftsmen, for example—and exploited new commercial opportunities to become very wealthy. Once they were rich, they tried to behave like the nobility. Many became patrons of the arts and leaders of society. Cosimo de Medici (1389–

1464), the ruler of Florence, came from a family of bankers and merchants. He was a great patron of artists and scholars, and was internationally respected as a diplomat and business-man. Merchants were living proof that civilized status could be acquired and did not have to be inherited.

GULF BETWEEN RICH AND POOR

Displays of wealth were increasingly used to emphasize the gulf between the elite and ordinary people. Vast accumulations of material goods—from astronomical instruments and rare books to exotic animals, fine textiles, and precious stones—were evidence of wealth and status. Sometimes the rich went to extreme lengths in their display of their wealth; in the 1550s Gaspare Ducci, an Italian merchant, gave a dinner for Mary of Austria, governor of the Netherlands, at which he served gold-plated oysters.

At the other end of the social scale were the majority of people—the laboring peasants. In eastern Europe in the 16th century peasants were tied to the service of their lord, sometimes working for him for several days a week. They were forbidden to travel, had no chance for education, and were very poor. They had virtually no opportunity to rise above their station.

By the 16th century in many parts of western Europe, however, peasants, though also very poor, were legally free. They were able to buy land, sell their own produce, and get some access to education. An ambitious peasant could therefore escape from the position he was born in. He could buy land, employ laborers, and make profits on his goods. He could buy an education for his sons, who could become apprentices, priests, or lawyers.

In towns and cities the status of craftsmen was respected and jealously

Below: A 16th-century painting showing Cardinal Thomas Wolsey (in red robes) confronting Sir Thomas More (in black) in 1529. Wolsey was a good example of how a talented and ambitious man could rise up the social order through the church. Born the son of a butcher, he became the most powerful man at the court of the English king Henry VIII (1491–1547).

guarded. It was very hard to become a member of a craftsmen's guild—often it was only possible by inheritance or marriage. In the guilds there was also a strict hierarchy of master craftsman, journeyman, and apprentice. The ordinary craftsmen, the journeymen, sold their labor on a daily basis, which meant that they had no job security and were always in a financially risky position. In many cities master craftsmen could gain municipal status, which meant they were involved in local government and responsible for law and order.

HOUSEHOLDS OF CULTURE

Many wealthy people in the big cities maintained large households, employing a great number of servants and groups of musicians, sculptors, and artists. Michelangelo used to boast that

he had always worked for noble patrons. He was proud that he was no longer considered, like many Renaissance artists, a tradesman, but had become a gentleman in service. By joining a noble household, he had ceased to be a mere artisan.

Above: A 15th-century fresco (wall painting) showing the inside of a grocer's shop. The increase in commerce and trade during the Renaissance period meant that there were many more opportunities for tradesmen to become wealthy.

MANNERS MAKETH THE MAN

The increased intermingling of people from very different backgrounds led to a new emphasis on manners. Knowing the correct way to behave in all circumstances could save the ambitious social climber from embarrassment. Throughout the 16th century a number of "self-improvement" books were published to teach the ignorant good manners. In 1530 the humanist thinker Erasmus published *De Civilitae* ("On Manners"). It was a hugely successful work that made the revolutionary assumption that good behavior could be taught, and that it was possible for everyone—regardless of their social origins—to acquire good manners. On the other hand, Baldassare Castiglione's *Il Cortegiano* ("The Courtier," 1528) was written by a man of aristocratic birth who was also a soldier, diplomat, and man of letters. His book was aimed at his social equals throughout Europe. While Castiglione believed that good birth was the main qualification for the courtier, he emphasized that education and ease of manner were essential attributes for advancement at court.

In 1558 the Italian Giovanni Della Casa published *Galateo*, which was subsequently translated into French, Latin, Spanish, German, and English. This popular guide to manners was specifically aimed at people who had recently become rich and was full of sensible advice. Della Casa covered all kinds of social behavior, from table manners to conversation and bodily functions: "When you have blown your nose, you should not open your handkerchief and inspect it, as though pearls or rubies had dropped out of your skull."

SEE ALSO

♦ Daily Life
♦ Dress
♦ Education
♦ Guilds and Crafts
♦ Merchants
♦ Population
♦ Poverty
♦ Wealth

Spain

In the 15th and 16th centuries the separate kingdoms of Spain were gradually united under a single crown to become the most powerful country in Europe. After the last part of Spain still under the control of the Muslim Moors was reconquered at the end of the 15th century, Spain went on to build a vast overseas empire in the New World. The country enjoyed a cultural golden age and was the leading defender of the Catholic church.

The marriage of Isabella of Castile (1451–1504) to Ferdinand V of Aragon (1452–1516) in 1469 was the first step toward a united Spain, creating a joint monarchy ruling over both kingdoms from 1479. Ferdinand and Isabella reestablished law and order in Aragon and Castile after many years of civil war. Royal power was reinforced by reforming the legal system, using a body of professional government officials such as lawyers rather than nobles, reducing the power of the nobility, and setting up the Inquisition.

THE SPANISH INQUISITION

The Inquisition was one of the most distinctive features of 16th-century Spain. This church tribunal was authorized by the pope to seek out and punish heretics (people whose religious ideas were different from those of the church). Penalties ranged from imprisonment to burning at the stake. The Inquisition was first used in 1478 against the *conversos* (Jewish converts to Catholicism), who were accused of secretly practicing their old faith. Later it was extended to all Christians.

In 1492 Christian Spain finally reconquered Granada, the last part of Spain still in the hands of the Muslim Moors, who had invaded from North Africa during the eighth century. Once Granada was secured, Isabella was able to sponsor Christopher Columbus's epic voyage to the Americas. The Catholic monarchs, as Ferdinand and

Above: A page from a 15th-century prayer book owned by Queen Joanna "the Mad," showing Joanna (center) with her parents, King Ferdinand of Aragon and Queen Isabella of Castile.

Right: A map showing Spain and the extent of the Spanish Empire in the New World in the late 16th century.

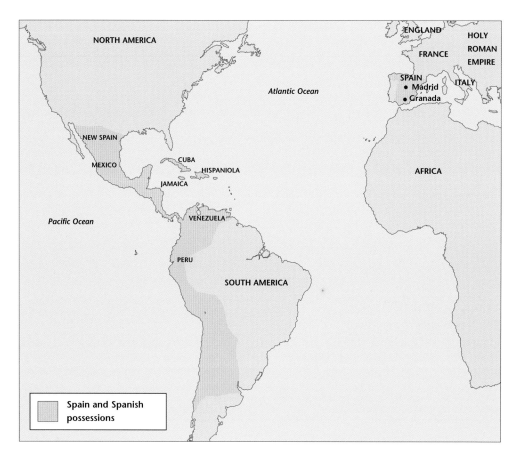

NORTH AMERICA

NEW SPAIN

MEXICO

CUBA

HISPANIOLA

JAMAICA

Pacific Ocean

VENEZUELA

PERU

SOUTH AMERICA

Atlantic Ocean

ENGLAND

FRANCE

SPAIN
● Madrid
● Granada

HOLY
ROMAN
EMPIRE

ITALY

AFRICA

Spain and Spanish
possessions

Isabella became known, sent out ambassadors across Europe. They also made strategic marriage alliances with England by marrying their daughter Catherine of Aragon to Henry VIII and with the Holy Roman Empire by marrying another daughter, Joanna "the Mad," to the emperor's son Philip.

The battle-hardened troops who had fought the Moors in Granada were a formidable force, and Spain soon became the major military power in southern Europe. When the French threatened Spanish territories in Italy in 1495, Spain formed an alliance, called the Holy League, with the Holy Roman emperor and expelled the French army from Naples. The addition of the counties of Cerdagne and Roussillon to the crown of Aragon in 1493, and of Navarre to Castile in 1515, brought extra security to Spain's northern frontier.

The conquest of the Aztecs of Mexico by the Spanish conquistador Hernán Cortés from 1519 to 1521 and of the Incas of Peru by Francisco Pizarro in 1531 and 1532 marked a spectacular expansion into the Americas. By the mid-16th century Spain held nominal control over a large part of South and Central America, Mexico, the Caribbean, and the Philippines (its main trading center in Asia).

Spain's colonial enterprise had two aims: to obtain treasure (silver and gold) and to establish settlements in the new territories. The crown attracted colonists to its American possessions through the *encomienda* system, which gave settlers land and Native American labor to work it in return for military service.

Spain's rise in political importance was not matched by a similar growth in its economy, which had been badly

CHRISTOPHER COLUMBUS

During the 15th century both Portugal and the kingdom of Castile were eager to find new sea routes to Asia in order to exploit its legendary wealth. After Portugal discovered the eastern sea route around the southern tip of Africa, Queen Isabella of Castile sponsored the Genoese navigator Christopher Columbus (1451–1506) to find a westward route to China via Japan. She hoped to use the profits she expected to make from the expedition to help recapture Jerusalem from the Muslims.

Columbus's discovery of the Americas on October 12, 1492, was accidental—it just happened that the West Indies lay roughly where Columbus was expecting to find Japan. During the course of three more voyages Columbus established a Spanish colony on Hispaniola (present-day Haiti and the Dominican Republic) and "discovered" the American mainland by landing in Venezuela. These discoveries paved the way for a Spanish Empire that stretched across almost the entire New World.

They also brought a conflict of interest between Castile and Portugal, which was settled by the Treaty of Tordesillas in 1494. Drawn up by the pope, this treaty divided the non-Christian world along an imaginary line 1,100 miles (1,760km) west of the Cape Verde Islands. Castile claimed all new lands to the west, while Portugal claimed all new lands to the east, which included Asia and all of Brazil.

Below: The Alhambra palace and fortress in Granada, which were built by the Muslim Moors. Ferdinand and Isabella conquered Granada in 1492, finally uniting all of Spain under their rule.

affected in 1492 by the expulsion of the Jews, many of whom were businessmen and traders. Most of the land in Spain belonged to the nobility, the crown, or the church and was used to raise sheep for the profitable wool trade rather than for growing food. By the mid-16th century Spain had to import grain to feed its growing population. Most of the enormous wealth from the New World was spent on military campaigns rather than developing Spain's economy.

Spain's transformation into western Europe's most powerful state began in 1516 with the reign of Charles I, Ferdinand's grandson, who later became the Holy Roman emperor Charles V, and continued under Charles' son Philip II. Throughout the 16th century Spain was ruled by a system of specialized councils that advised the king on military, religious, and financial policy and on territorial matters. The crown strongly supported the Catholic church and championed the cause of the Counter Reformation

against the spread of Protestantism across Europe. Spanish culture also flourished during this time. A number of universities became leading centers of the latest humanist learning, including Salamanca and the newly founded university of Alcalá de Henares. In the 16th century a number of writers, artists, and architects introduced Renaissance ideas to Spain. They included the novelist Miguel de Cervantes (1547–1616) and the painter El Greco (1541–1614). An enthusiasm for Renaissance architecture led to many new buildings, including Philip II's monastic palace, El Escorial, near Madrid, which was completed in 1584.

Below: A 16th-century portrait of Charles I of Spain as a young man. He became the Holy Roman emperor Charles V and the most powerful ruler in Europe.

CHARLES V

When Ferdinand of Aragon died in 1516, his grandson Charles (1500–1558) inherited a united Spain. Three years later he was elected Holy Roman emperor as Charles V, making him the most powerful ruler in Europe. As well as his Spanish empire, Charles controlled the Burgundian inheritance, which included the Netherlands, where he was brought up, the Austrian Hapsburg territories, and Germany.

Charles' duties as emperor meant that he spent little time in Spain, which displeased his Spanish subjects. They were also angry that he gave important positions of power to non-Spaniards and that they had to pay high taxes. In 1520 this resentment led to a revolt of the *comuneros* (town governments), which Charles was only able to crush with the help of the nobles. However, he later became more popular with his Spanish subjects, who began to take pride in Spain's imperial achievements.

Charles' vast territories brought him political and military power, but also powerful enemies, including the French king, Francis I. During his reign Charles was almost continuously at war with France—mainly over Italy—as well as with the German Protestant princes and the Ottoman Turks.

PHILIP II

In 1555 Charles abdicated, exhausted by his constant fighting, and divided his lands between his son Philip, who received everything except Germany, and his brother Ferdinand, who

SPANISH ART

Spanish art in this period was influenced by developments in Italy and the Netherlands. The two main artists were the sculptor Alonso Berruguete (1488–1561) and the painter Domenikos Theotokopoulos (1541–1614), known as El Greco ("The Greek"). Berruguete was a painter as well as the leading sculptor of polychromed (painted) wood. He trained in Italy and was known as the "Spanish Michelangelo." His masterpiece was the high altar of the Church of San Benito in Valladolid.

El Greco was born in Crete and studied with the Venetian painter Titian before moving in 1570 to Toledo in Spain, then one of the greatest religious centers in Catholic Europe and the headquarters of the Counter Reformation. Most of El Greco's paintings were commissioned by the church for the interiors of the city's cathedral, churches, and religious establishments. They show Byzantine and Venetian influences, in addition to his own highly personal style, which was characterized by the use of elongated forms and light and color to convey spiritual feeling. His most famous work is *The Burial of Count Orgaz* (1586), one of the finest group portraits of the 16th century, which mixes religious and secular themes, reflecting the influence of Catholicism on Spanish life.

Above: El Greco's most famous painting, **The Burial of Count Orgaz,** *painted in 1586.*

received Germany and became Holy Roman emperor. This division caused major problems for Philip II (1527–1598) because it exposed Spain's shortcomings as an independent power. To compensate, Philip tripled the size of Spain's army, borrowing a large amount of money to pay for it.

A GREAT POWER

Under Philip Spain became a great power. Philip seized the chance to annex Portugal in 1580, uniting the whole peninsula for the first time. Like his father, Philip considered himself to be the leader of the Catholic world and put all his resources into defending Catholicism. Philip's attempts at enforcing religious unity across his empire caused much resentment. His

repression of the Dutch Protestant rebels in 1566 sparked a costly revolt that lasted for 80 years. However, the victory of a combined Spanish, Venetian, and papal fleet over the Ottoman Turks at Lepanto in 1571 ended Turkish expansion in Europe and confirmed Spain as the champion of the Catholic church.

THE END OF AN ERA

Despite the achievements during the reign of Philip II and the vast wealth that poured in from the Spanish colonies, by the late 1590s Spain was in crisis. The countryside was devastated by crop failures, cities were swept by plague, and the country was bankrupt after the cost of so much warfare had left it crippled with debt.

SEE ALSO

♦ Americas
♦ Catholic Church
♦ Cervantes
♦ Charles V
♦ Counter Reformation
♦ Exploration
♦ France
♦ Hapsburg Family
♦ Holy Roman Empire
♦ Inquisition
♦ Netherlands
♦ Ottoman Empire
♦ Philip II
♦ Portugal
♦ Wealth

Tapestry

A tapestry is a type of woven fabric made on a loom. It is made from a set of plain threads running vertically (called warps) in between which colored threads running horizontally (called wefts) are woven to create patterns and pictures. Tapestries have been made by many different cultures since ancient times, but some of the best-known examples were woven from the 14th to 16th centuries in the present-day countries of France and Belgium.

Tapestries began to be woven in the countries of northern Europe as wall hangings to keep out drafts in cold, damp castles. In the 16th century the fashion spread to the warmer countries of southern Europe. Many tapestries were very large, designed to cover a whole wall, and they were often made in sets. Tapestries also became popular for smaller furnishings, such as cushion covers and hangings for beds.

STATUS SYMBOLS

Besides their practical function of keeping rooms warm, tapestries were highly regarded as works of art. They were often more costly than paintings, and wealthy rulers assembled huge collections. The English king Henry VIII, for example, had about 2,000 tapestries in his royal collection when he died in 1547.

Left: One of a set of six tapestries known as the "Lady and the Unicorn Tapestries" made at the end of the 15th century. They were designed in France and woven in the Netherlands. The background is designed with mille fleurs ("a thousand flowers"), a highly decorative pattern that was popular from the 14th century onward.

Because of their costliness tapestries were great status symbols. They often showed traditional subjects such as scenes of courtly life packed full of details like sumptuous clothing, plants, and animals; but sometimes they were also specially created to celebrate particular individuals or their achievements. In the 16th century the Holy Roman emperor Charles V ordered several sets of tapestries to celebrate his military victories.

MATERIALS AND METHODS

Tapestries were very expensive because of the materials they were made from and the time and skill required to weave them. Wool was the most common thread used in medieval and Renaissance tapestries, but silk was also widely incorporated for fine details and subtle colors like skin tones. The most magnificent tapestries also had threads made from silver and gold.

Tapestry weavers were highly skilled, and their work was time-consuming—it could take up to a month to weave 10 square feet (1 sq.m) of a complicated pattern. Several weavers often worked side by side on a tapestry, basing their design on a full-size colored drawing called a "cartoon," which had been made by a painter.

TAPESTRY-MAKING CENTERS

Because of the expense and time involved in making tapestries, a stable political climate and wealthy patrons (the people who ordered and bought artworks) were required. The first great medieval and Renaissance tapestry centers grew up around the prosperous French and Burgundian courts in the 14th and 15th centuries. During the 14th century the French cities of Paris and Arras were the most important. In the 15th century, however, when France

was torn by warfare, Flanders (in present-day Belgium) took the lead in tapestry making, with Tournai and Brussels also becoming major centers.

During the Renaissance Flemish weavers became so renowned for the quality of their workmanship that when wealthy Italian patrons wanted tapestries, they often had them made in Brussels or brought Flemish weavers to Italy. In 1515, for example, Pope Leo X commissioned a series of 10 tapestries illustrating the lives of Saint Peter and Saint Paul for the Sistine Chapel in the Vatican. The cartoons were designed by the Italian artist Raphael in 1515–1516 and sent to Brussels, where tapestries were woven from them in the workshop of Pieter van Aelst.

As a result of the religious unrest and civil war into which the Netherlands was plunged in the second half of the 16th century, many weavers fled. Brussels remained a major center for tapestry production, but many weavers went abroad as kings and rulers across Europe tried to attract them to their courts. They went to Germany, Italy, Spain, and Paris, which in the 17th century once again became a major tapestry-making center.

Above: **Saint Paul Preaching at the Synagogue,** *one of 10 tapestries woven in Brussels to designs made by Raphael in 1515–1516. Until this time tapestries had been quite old-fashioned in design; but after Flemish weavers saw Raphael's cartoons, their work was influenced by the latest developments taking place in Italian art.*

SEE ALSO

♦ Decorative Arts
♦ Dress
♦ Raphael
♦ Textiles

Timeline

♦ **1305** Giotto begins work on frescoes for the Arena Chapel, Padua—he is often considered the father of Renaissance art.

♦ **1321** Dante publishes the *Divine Comedy*, which has a great influence on later writers.

♦ **1327** Petrarch begins writing the sonnets known as the *Canzoniere*.

♦ **1337** The start of the Hundred Years' War between England and France.

♦ **1353** Boccaccio writes the *Decameron*, an influential collection of 100 short stories.

♦ **1368** The Ming dynasty comes to power in China.

♦ **1377** Pope Gregory XI moves the papacy back to Rome from Avignon, where it has been based since 1309.

♦ **1378** The Great Schism begins: two popes, Urban VI and Clement VII, both lay claim to the papacy.

♦ **1378** English theologian John Wycliffe criticizes the practices of the Roman Catholic church.

♦ **1380** Ivan I of Muscovy defeats the army of the Mongol Golden Horde at the battle of Kulikovo.

♦ **1389** The Ottomans defeat the Serbs at the battle of Kosovo, beginning a new phase of Ottoman expansion.

♦ **1397** Sigismund of Hungary is defeated by the Ottoman Turks at the battle of Nicopolis.

♦ **1397** Queen Margaret of Denmark unites Denmark, Sweden, and Norway under the Union of Kalmar.

♦ **1398** The Mongol leader Tamerlane invades India.

♦ **1399** Henry Bolingbroke becomes Henry IV of England.

♦ **1400** English writer Geoffrey Chaucer dies, leaving his *Canterbury Tales* unfinished.

♦ **1403** In Italy the sculptor Ghiberti wins a competition to design a new set of bronze doors for Florence Cathedral.

♦ **c.1402** The Bohemian preacher Jan Hus begins to attack the corruption of the church.

♦ **1405** The Chinese admiral Cheng Ho commands the first of seven expeditions to the Indian Ocean and East Africa.

♦ **1415** Jan Hus is summoned to the Council of Constance and condemned to death.

♦ **1415** Henry V leads the English to victory against the French at the battle of Agincourt.

♦ **c.1415** Florentine sculptor Donatello produces his sculpture *Saint George*.

♦ **1416** Venice defeats the Ottoman fleet at the battle of Gallipoli, but does not check the Ottoman advance.

♦ **1417** The Council of Constance elects Martin V pope, ending the Great Schism.

♦ **1418** Brunelleschi designs the dome of Florence Cathedral.

♦ **1420** Pope Martin V returns the papacy to Rome, bringing peace and order to the city.

♦ **c.1420** Prince Henry of Portugal founds a school of navigation at Sagres, beginning a great age of Portuguese exploration.

♦ **1422** Charles VI of France dies, leaving his throne to the English king Henry VI. Charles VI's son also claims the throne.

♦ **c.1425** Florentine artist Masaccio paints the *Holy Trinity*, the first painting to use the new science of perspective.

♦ **1429** Joan of Arc leads the French to victory at Orléans; Charles VII is crowned king of France in Reims Cathedral.

♦ **1431** The English burn Joan of Arc at the stake for heresy.

♦ **1433** Sigismund of Luxembourg becomes Holy Roman emperor.

♦ **1434** Cosimo de Medici comes to power in Florence.

♦ **1434** The Flemish artist Jan van Eyck paints the *Arnolfini Marriage* using the newly developed medium of oil paint.

♦ **1439** The Council of Florence proclaims the reunion of the Western and Orthodox churches.

♦ **c.1440** Donatello completes his statue of David—the first life-size bronze sculpture since antiquity.

♦ **1443** Federigo da Montefeltro becomes ruler of Urbino.

♦ **1447** The Milanese people declare their city a republic.

♦ **1450** The condottiere Francesco Sforza seizes control of Milan.

♦ **1450** Fra Angelico paints *The Annunciation* for the monastery of San Marco in Florence.

♦ **1453** Constantinople, capital of the Byzantine Empire, falls to the Ottomans and becomes the capital of the Muslim Empire.

♦ **1453** The French defeat the English at the battle of Castillon, ending the Hundred Years' War.

♦ **1454–1456** Venice, Milan, Florence, Naples, and the papacy form the Italian League to maintain peace in Italy.

♦ **1455** The start of the Wars of the Roses between the Houses of York and Lancaster in England.

♦ **c.1455** The German Johannes Gutenberg develops the first printing press using movable type.

♦ **1456** The Florentine painter Uccello begins work on the *Battle of San Romano*.

♦ **1461** The House of York wins the Wars of the Roses; Edward IV becomes king of England.

♦ **1461** Sonni Ali becomes king of the Songhai Empire in Africa.

♦ **1462** Marsilio Ficino founds the Platonic Academy of Florence— the birthplace of Renaissance Neoplatonism.

♦ **1463** War breaks out between Venice and the Ottoman Empire.

♦ **1465** The Italian painter Mantegna begins work on the Camera degli Sposi in Mantua.

♦ **1467** Civil war breaks out in Japan, lasting for over a century.

♦ **1469** Lorenzo the Magnificent, grandson of Cosimo de Medici, comes to power in Florence.

♦ **1469** The marriage of Isabella I of Castile and Ferdinand V of Aragon unites the two kingdoms.

♦ **1470** The Florentine sculptor Verrocchio completes his *David*.

♦ **1476** William Caxton establishes the first English printing press at Westminster, near London.

♦ **1477** Pope Sixtus IV begins building the Sistine Chapel.

♦ **c.1477** Florentine painter Sandro Botticelli paints the *Primavera*, one of the first large-scale mythological paintings of the Renaissance.

♦ **1478** The Spanish Inquisition is founded in Spain.

♦ **1480** The Ottoman fleet destroys the port of Otranto in south Italy.

♦ **1485** Henry Tudor becomes Henry VII of England—the start of the Tudor dynasty.

♦ **1486** *The Witches' Hammer* is published, a handbook on how to hunt down witches.

♦ **1488** Portuguese navigator Bartholomeu Dias reaches the Cape of Good Hope.

♦ **1491** Missionaries convert King Nzina Nkowu of the Congo to Christianity.

♦ **1492** The Spanish monarchs conquer Granada, the last Moorish territory in Spain.

♦ **1492** Christopher Columbus lands in the Bahamas, claiming the territory for Spain.

♦ **1492** Henry VII of England renounces all English claims to the French throne.

♦ **1493** The Hapsburg Maximilian becomes Holy Roman emperor.

♦ **1494** Charles VIII of France invades Italy, beginning four decades of Italian wars.

♦ **1494** In Italy Savonarola comes to power in Florence.

♦ **1494** The Treaty of Tordesillas divides the non-Christian world between Spain and Portugal.

♦ **1495** Leonardo da Vinci begins work on *The Last Supper* .

♦ **1495** Spain forms a Holy League with the Holy Roman emperor and expels the French from Naples.

♦ **1498** Portuguese navigator Vasco da Gama reaches Calicut, India.

♦ **1498** German artist Dürer creates the *Apocalypse* woodcuts.

♦ **1500** Portuguese navigator Pedro Cabral discovers Brazil.

♦ **c.1500–1510** Dutch painter Hieronymous Bosch paints *The Garden of Earthly Delights*.

♦ **c.1502** Italian architect Donato Bramante designs the Tempietto Church in Rome.

♦ **1503** Leonardo da Vinci begins painting the *Mona Lisa*.

♦ **1504** Michelangelo finishes his statue of David, widely seen as a symbol of Florence.

♦ **c.1505** Venetian artist Giorgione paints *The Tempest*.

♦ **1506** The Italian architect Donato Bramante begins work on rebuilding Saint Peter's, Rome.

♦ **1508** Michelangelo begins work on the ceiling of the Sistine Chapel in the Vatican.

♦ **1509** Henry VIII ascends the throne of England.

♦ **1509** The League of Cambrai defeats Venice at the battle of Agnadello.

♦ **1510–1511** Raphael paints *The School of Athens* in the Vatican.

♦ **1511** The French are defeated at the battle of Ravenna in Italy and are forced to retreat over the Alps.

♦ **1513** Giovanni de Medici becomes Pope Leo X.

♦ **1515** Thomas Wolsey becomes lord chancellor of England.

♦ **1515** Francis I becomes king of France. He invades Italy and captures Milan.

♦ **c.1515** German artist Grünewald paints the *Isenheim Altarpiece.*

♦ **1516** Charles, grandson of the emperor Maximilian I, inherits the Spanish throne as Charles I.

♦ **1516** Thomas More publishes his political satire *Utopia.*

♦ **1516** Dutch humanist Erasmus publishes a more accurate version of the Greek New Testament.

♦ **1517** Martin Luther pins his 95 theses on the door of the castle church in Wittenburg.

♦ **1519** Charles I of Spain becomes Holy Roman emperor Charles V.

♦ **1519–1521** Hernán Cortés conquers Mexico for Spain.

♦ **1520** Henry VIII of England and Francis I of France meet at the Field of the Cloth of Gold to sign a treaty of friendship.

♦ **1520** Portuguese navigator Ferdinand Magellan discovers a route to the Indies around the tip of South America.

♦ **1520** Süleyman the Magnificent becomes ruler of the Ottoman Empire, which now dominates the eastern Mediterranean.

♦ **1520–1523** Titian paints *Bacchus and Ariadne* for Alfonso d'Este.

♦ **1521** Pope Leo X excommuicates Martin Luther.

♦ **1521** The emperor Charles V attacks France, beginning a long period of European war.

♦ **1522** Ferdinand Magellan's ship the *Victoria* is the first to sail around the world.

♦ **1523–1525** Huldrych Zwingli sets up a Protestant church at Zurich in Switzerland.

♦ **1525** In Germany the Peasants' Revolt is crushed, and its leader, Thomas Münzer, is executed.

♦ **1525** The emperor Charles V defeats the French at the battle of Pavia and takes Francis I prisoner.

♦ **1525** William Tyndale translates the New Testament into English.

♦ **1526** The Ottoman Süleyman the Magnificent defeats Hungary at the battle of Mohács.

♦ **1526** Muslim Mongol leader Babur invades northern India and establishes the Mogul Empire.

♦ **c.1526** The Italian artist Correggio paints the *Assumption of the Virgin* in Parma Cathedral.

♦ **1527** Charles V's armies overrun Italy and sack Rome.

♦ **1527–1530** Gustavus I founds a Lutheran state church in Sweden.

♦ **1528** Italian poet and humanist Baldassare Castiglione publishes *The Courtier.*

♦ **1529** The Ottoman Süleyman the Magnificent lays siege to Vienna, but eventually retreats.

♦ **1530** The Catholic church issues the "Confutation," attacking Luther and Protestantism.

♦ **1531** The Protestant princes of Germany form the Schmalkaldic League.

♦ **1531–1532** Francisco Pizarro conquers Peru for Spain.

♦ **1532** Machiavelli's *The Prince* is published after his death.

♦ **1533** Henry VIII of England rejects the authority of the pope and marries Anne Boleyn.

♦ **1533** Anabaptists take over the city of Münster in Germany.

♦ **1533** Christian III of Denmark founds the Lutheran church of Denmark.

♦ **1534** Paul III becomes pope and encourages the growth of new religious orders such as the Jesuits.

♦ **1534** Luther publishes his German translation of the Bible.

♦ **1534** The Act of Supremacy declares Henry VIII supreme head of the Church of England.

♦ **c.1535** Parmigianino paints the mannerist masterpiece *Madonna of the Long Neck.*

♦ **1535–1536** The Swiss city of Geneva becomes Protestant and expels the Catholic clergy.

♦ **1536** Calvin publishes *Institutes of the Christian Religion,* which sets out his idea of predestination.

♦ **1536** Pope Paul III sets up a reform commission to examine the state of the Catholic church.

♦ **1537** Hans Holbein is appointed court painter to Henry VIII of England.

♦ **1539** Italian painter Bronzino begins working for Cosimo de Medici the Younger in Florence.

♦ **1539** Ignatius de Loyola founds the Society of Jesus (the Jesuits).

♦ **1541** John Calvin sets up a model Christian city in Geneva.

♦ **1543** Andreas Vesalius publishes *On the Structure of the Human Body,* a handbook of anatomy based on dissections.

♦ **1543** Polish astronomer Copernicus's *On the Revolutions of the Heavenly Spheres* proposes a sun-centered universe.

♦ **1544** Charles V and Francis I of France sign the Truce of Crespy.

♦ **1545** Pope Paul III organizes the Council of Trent to counter the threat of Protestantism.

♦ **1545** Spanish explorers find huge deposits of silver in the Andes Mountains of Peru.

♦ **1547** Charles V defeats the Protestant Schmalkaldic League at the Battle of Mühlberg.

♦ **1547** Ivan IV "the Terrible" declares himself czar of Russia.

♦ **1548** Titian paints the equestrian portrait *Charles V after the Battle of Mühlberg.*

♦ **1548** Tintoretto paints *Saint Mark Rescuing the Slave.*

♦ **1550** Italian Georgio Vasari publishes his *Lives of the Artists.*

♦ **1553** Mary I of England restores the Catholic church.

♦ **1554** Work begins on the Cathedral of Saint Basil in Red Square, Moscow.

♦ **1555** At the Peace of Augsburg Charles V allows the German princes to determine their subjects' religion.

♦ **1556** Ivan IV defeats the last Mongol khanates. Muscovy now dominates the Volga region.

♦ **1556** Philip II becomes king of Spain.

♦ **1559** Elizabeth I of England restores the Protestant church.

♦ **1562** The Wars of Religion break out in France.

♦ **1565** Flemish artist Pieter Bruegel the Elder paints *Hunters in the Snow.*

♦ **1565** Italian architect Palladio designs the Villa Rotunda, near Vicenza.

♦ **1566** The Dutch revolt against the Spanish over the loss of political and religious freedoms:

Philip II of Spain sends 10,000 troops under the duke of Alba to suppress the revolt.

♦ **1569** Flemish cartographer Mercator produces a world map using a new projection.

♦ **1571** Philip II of Spain and an allied European force defeat the Ottomans at the battle of Lepanto.

♦ **1572** In Paris, France, a Catholic mob murders thousands of Huguenots in the Saint Bartholomew's Day Massacre.

♦ **1572** Danish astronomer Tycho Brahe sees a new star.

♦ **1573** Venetian artist Veronese paints the *Feast of the House of Levi.*

♦ **1579** The seven northern provinces of the Netherlands form the Union of Utrecht.

♦ **1580** Giambologna creates his mannerist masterpiece *Flying Mercury.*

♦ **1585** Henry III of France bans Protestantism in France; civil war breaks out again in the War of the Three Henrys.

♦ **1586** El Greco, a Greek artist active in Spain, paints the *Burial of Count Orgaz.*

♦ **1587** Mary, Queen of Scots, is executed by Elizabeth I of England.

♦ **c.1587** Nicholas Hilliard paints the miniature *Young Man among Roses.*

♦ **1588** Philip II of Spain launches his great Armada against England —but the fleet is destroyed.

♦ **1589** Henry of Navarre becomes king of France as Henry IV.

♦ **1592–1594** Tintoretto paints *The Last Supper.*

♦ **1596** Edmund Spencer publishes the *Faerie Queene,* glorifying Elizabeth I as "Gloriana."

♦ **1598** Henry IV of France grants Huguenots and Catholics equal political rights.

♦ **1598** In England the Globe Theater is built on London's south bank; it stages many of Shakespeare's plays.

♦ **1600–1601** Caravaggio paints *The Crucifixion of Saint Peter,* an early masterpiece of baroque art.

♦ **1603** Elizabeth I of England dies and is succeeded by James I, son of Mary, Queen of Scots.

♦ **1610** Galileo's *The Starry Messenger* supports the sun-centered model of the universe.

♦ **1620** The Italian painter Artemisia Gentileschi paints *Judith and Holofernes.*

Glossary

A.D. The letters A.D. stand for the Latin Anno Domini, which means "in the year of our Lord." Dates with these letters written after them are measured forward from the year Christ was born.

Altarpiece A painting or sculpture placed behind an altar in a church.

Apprentice Someone (usually a young person) legally bound to a craftsman for a number of years in order to learn a craft.

Baptistery Part of a church, or a separate building, where people are baptized.

B.C. Short for "Before Christ." Dates with these letters after them are measured backward from the year of Christ's birth.

Bureaucracy A system of government that relies on a body of officials and usually involves much paperwork and many regulations.

Cardinal An official of the Catholic church, highest in rank below the pope. The cardinals elect the pope.

Chalice A drinking cup, often made of gold or silver, that is used in the church communion service.

Classical A term used to describe the civilizations of ancient Greece and Rome, and any later art and architecture based on ancient Greek and Roman examples.

Commission To order a specially made object, like a painting or tapestry.

Condottiere A mercenary soldier, that is, a soldier who will fight for anyone in return for money.

Connoisseur An expert in a particular fine art or in a matter of taste.

Contemporary Someone or something that exists at the same period of time.

Curia The various offices of the Vatican that help the pope in his work as head of the Catholic church.

Diet A general assembly of representatives of the Holy Roman empire who gathered to pass laws and make decisions.

Equestrian A term used to describe something relating to a person on horseback. For example, an equestrian sculpture is a sculpture portraying a soldier or leader on horseback.

Excommunicate To ban someone from taking part in the rites of the church.

Foreshortening A technique used by artists in their pictures to re-create the appearance of objects when seen from a particular angle. It involves shortening some measurements, according to the laws of perspective (see below), to make it look as if objects are projecting toward or receding away from the surface of the picture.

Fresco A type of painting that is usually used for decorating walls and ceilings in which colors are painted into wet plaster.

Guild An association of merchants or craftsmen organized to protect the interests of its members and to regulate the quality of their goods and services.

Heresy A belief that is contrary to the accepted teachings of the church.

Heretic Someone whose beliefs contradict those of the church.

Humanism A new way of thinking about human life that characterized the Renaissance. It was based on the study of the "humanities"—that is, ancient Greek and Roman texts, history, and philosophy—and stressed the importance of developing rounded, cultured people.

Humanist Someone who adopted humanism, the new way of thinking about human life that characterized the Renaissance.

Hundred Years' War A long-drawn-out war between France and England, lasting from 1337 to 1453. It consisted of a series of campaigns with periods of tense peace in between.

Journeyman A qualified craftsman who has completed his apprenticeship and works for another person on either a specific project or a daily basis.

Laity or lay people Anyone who is not a member of the clergy.

Mercenary A soldier who will fight for anyone in return for money.

Monopoly Exclusive rights or control over something.

Patron Someone who orders and pays for a work of art.

Patronage The act of ordering and paying for a work of art.

Pediment A term used in classical architecture to describe the triangular-shaped structure at the top of a building façade (front); the term is also used for moldings above windows and doorways.

Perspective A technique that allows artists to create the impression of three-dimensional space in their pictures. Nearby objects are made to appear larger, and far away objects are shown as smaller.

Portico A term used in classical architecture to describe a roofed structure with columns and a pediment (see above) on the front of a building; also known as a temple front.

Propaganda The spreading of ideas or information, which may be true or false, in order to help a particular cause or person.

Tempera A type of paint made by mixing powdered pigments (colors) with egg. Tempera was widely used by painters in medieval times and the Renaissance.

Treatise A book or long essay laying down the principles, or rules, of a particular subject.

Vatican The headquarters of the pope and papal government in Rome.

Vernacular The language of the ordinary people of a country, rather than a literary or formal language, such as Latin.

Further Reading

Anderson, James Maxwell. *Daily Life During the Spanish Inquisition.* Westport, CT: Greenwood Publishing, 2002.

Baxandall, Michael. *Limewood Sculptors of Renaissance Germany.* New Haven, CT: Yale University Press, 1982.

Beeching, Jack. *The Galleys at Lepanto.* New York: Scribner's, 1983.

Bobrick, Benson. *Fearful Majesty: The Life and Reign of Ivan the Terrible.* New York: Putnam, 1987.

Brown, Beverly Louise. *The Genius of Rome 1592–1623.* New York: Harry N. Abrams, 2001.

Chambers, James. *Devil's Horsemen: The Mongol Invasion of Europe.* London: Phoenix Press, 2001.

Clare, John D. *Italian Renaissance.* San Diego, CA: Harcourt Brace, 1995.

Codye, Corinn. *Queen Isabella I.* Austin, TX: Raintree/Steck Vaughn, 1989.

Cole, Alison. *Eyewitness: Renaissance.* New York: DK Publishing, 2000.

Corrick, James A. *The Renaissance.* San Diego, CA: Lucent Books, 1998.

De Vecchi, Pierluigi. *Michelangelo: The Vatican Frescoes.* New York: Abbeville Press, 1997.

Delmarcel, Guy. *Flemish Tapestry.* New York: Harry N. Abrams, 2000.

Di Niscemi, Maita. *Manor Houses and Castles of Sweden: A Voyage through Five Centuries.* New York: Scala Books, 1994.

Drury, John. *Painting the Word: Christian Pictures and Their Meanings.* New Haven, CT: Yale University Press, 1999.

Erlanger, Rachel. *The Unarmed Prophet: Savonarola in Florence.* New York: McGraw-Hill, 1987.

Gardiner, Robert. *Cogs, Caravels and Galleons: The Sailing Ship 1000–1650.* Edison, NJ: Chartwell Books, 2000.

Greenhill, Wendy, and Paul Wignall. *Shakespeare: Man of the Theater.* Chicago, IL: Heinemann Library, 2000.

Hersey, George L. *High Renaissance Art in St. Peter's and the Vatican: An Interpretive Guide.* Chicago, IL: University of Chicago Press, 1993.

Howarth, David. *Voyage of the Armada: The Spanish Story.* New York: Penguin, 1982.

January, Brendan. *Science in the Renaissance.* New York: Franklin Watts, 1999.

Lubkin, Gregory. *A Renaissance Court: Milan under Galeazzo Maria Sforza.* Berkeley, CA: University of California Press, 1994.

MacDonald, Fiona. *Drake and the Armada.* New York: Hampstead Press, 1988.

Martin, Lillian Ray. *The Art and Archaeology of Venetian Ships and Boats.* College Station, TX: Texas A&M University Press, 2001.

McHam, Sarah Blake. *Looking at Italian Renaissance Sculpture.* Cambridge, UK: Cambridge University Press, 1998.

Millar, Heather. *Spain in the Age of Exploration.* New York: Benchmark Books, 1999.

Milner-Gulland, Robin. *The Russians.* Oxford: Blackwell Publishers, 1997.

Moorman, John. *History of the Franciscan Order: From Its Origins to the Year 1517.* Oxford: Clarendon Press, 1968.

Morgan, David. *The Mongols.* Oxford: Blackwell Publishers, 1990.

Morley, Jacqueline. *Shakespeare's Theater.* New York: Peter Bedrick Books, 1994.

Morrison, Taylor. *Neptune Fountain: The Apprenticeship of a Renaissance Sculptor.* New York: Holiday House, 1997.

Nesbit, Edith. *The Children's Shakespeare.* Chicago, IL: Academy Chicago Publishers, 2000.

O'Donnell, Robert A. *Hooked on Philosophy: Thomas Aquinas Made Easy.* New York: Alba House, 1995.

Olson, Roberta J.M. *Italian Renaissance Sculpture.* London: Thames & Hudson, 1992.

Osman, Karen. *The Italian Renaissance.* San Diego, CA: Lucent Books, 1995.

Partridge, Loren. *Michelangelo: The Sistine Chapel Ceiling, Rome.* New York: George Braziller, 1996.

Partridge, Loren. *The Art of Renaissance Rome 1400–1600.* New York: Harry N. Abrams, 1996.

Poeschke, Joachim. *Michelangelo and His World: Sculpture of the Italian Renaissance.* New York: Harry N. Abrams, 1996.

Pope-Hennessy, John Wyndham. *Donatello: Sculptor.* New York: Abbeville Press, 1993.

Richmond, Robin. *Michelangelo and the Creation of the Sistine Chapel.* New York: Crescent Books, 1995.

Ridolfi, Roberto. *The Life of Girolamo Savonarola.* New York: Knopf, 1959.

Rosen, Michael. *William Shakespeare: His Work and His World.* Cambridge, MA: Candlewick Press, 2001.

Roth, Cecil. *Spanish Inquisition.* New York: W.W. Norton, 1996.

Scott, Franklin D. *Sweden: The Nation's History.* Carbondale, IL: Southern Illinois University Press, 1989

Shelland, Domenic. *William Shakespeare.* Oxford: Oxford University Press Children's Books, 2000.

Stewart, Gail B. *Life during the Spanish Inquisition.* San Diego, CA: Lucent Books, 1998.

Thomson, Francis Paul. *Tapestry: Mirror of History.* New York: Crown Publishers, 1981.

Tomlinson, Janis. *From El Greco to Goya: Painting in Spain, 1561–1828.* New York: Harry N. Abrams, 1997.

Trevelyan, George Macaulay. *England in the Age of Wycliffe.* New York: AMS Press, 1975.

Zickgraf, Ralph. *Sweden.* Broomall, PA: Chelsea House Publishing, 1997.

WEBSITES

World history site
www.historyworld.net

BBC Online: History
www.bbc.co.uk/history

The Webmuseum's tour of the Renaissance
www.oir.ucf.edu/wm/paint/glo/renaissance/

Virtual time travel tour of the Renaissance
library.thinkquest.org/3588/Renaissance/

The Renaissance
www.learner.org/exhibits/renaissance

National Gallery of Art—tour of 16th-century Italian paintings
www.nga.gov/collection/gallery/ita16.htm

Uffizi Art Gallery, Florence
musa.uffizi.firenze.it/welcomeE.html

Database of Renaissance artists
www.artcyclopedia.com/index.html

Set Index

Numbers in **bold type** are volume numbers.

Page numbers in *italics* refer to pictures or their captions.

MAPS
The maps in this book show the locations of cities, states, and empires of the
Renaissance period. However, for the sake of clarity, present-day place names are
often used.